"Imagine picking up a novel and only reading the middle! While the Bible is not like any other book, it is just as important to have a clear understanding of its beginning and end in order to understand God's story of redemption. Justin Miller's clear examination of this history through the lens of the Covenant of Works and the Covenant of Grace is to be commended as a helpful resource for any believer."

—SAM WALDRON, president, Covenant
Baptist Theological Seminary

"Justin Miller has done a great service to the church in writing this book. As a pastor, I've struggled to find a resource on covenant theology that would be profitable for both newly converted Christians and seasoned saints. Miller has surely written with that struggle in mind, taking a top-shelf understanding of God's covenant faithfulness and carefully placing it on the bottom shelf for the spiritual profit of every member of Christ's church."

—JASON GUNTER, pastor, First Baptist Church Willow Springs

"*Ruin and Redemption* is an excellent introduction to biblical theology. It captures the heart of the biblical storyline that runs from Genesis to Revelation—the gospel of Jesus Christ. Justin Miller provides us with the significant overarching themes and motifs of Scripture as they progress and develop throughout the history of redemption. There is so much substance in such a small book that it is one of the few books that are worthy of reading more than once."

—JEFFREY D. JOHNSON, President of
Grace Bible Theological Seminary

"In *Ruin and Redemption*, Justin Miller ably shows how Genesis 1–3 set the stage for the story of God's salvation. This little book is a veritable 'body of divinity,' and it provides a clear and concise overview of the gospel that's well-suited to ground the saints in the truth and introduce the nonbeliever to the good news that will set them free."

—ROBERT GONZALES JR., dean, Reformed Baptist Seminary

"*Ruin and Redemption* sketches the grand sweep of human history from paradise lost to paradise found. In essence, it is a compelling love story packed with the gripping elements of a foolish and helpless maiden, a savage and cruel dragon, an offended yet seeking father, along with a heroic and rescuing lover."

—**MARK CHANSKI**, coordinator, Reformed Baptist Network

Ruin and Redemption

Ruin and Redemption

A Study of the Covenant of Works and
Covenant of Grace from Genesis 2–3

JUSTIN MILLER

WIPF & STOCK · Eugene, Oregon

RUIN AND REDEMPTION
A Study of the Covenant of Works and Covenant of Grace from Genesis
2–3

Wipf & Stock
An Imprint of Wipf and Stock Publishers
199 W. 8th Ave., Suite 3
Eugene, OR 97401

www.wipfandstock.com

PAPERBACK ISBN: 978-1-6667-6043-9
HARDCOVER ISBN: 978-1-6667-6044-6
EBOOK ISBN: 978-1-6667-6045-3

12/23/22

JoDawn, my bride and ruthless editor. I love you.
Outside of the Lord Jesus and his saving my soul, you
are God's greatest gift to this unworthy man.

Pastor Calvin your faithfulness to under-shepherd a local
church for over thirty-eight years and your love of truth has
been a blessed exhortation unto faithfulness for me as a pastor.

Brother Ron your quiet endurance, love for truth,
and your fatherly wisdom is something I will
cherish in Christ Jesus for all my days.

Contents

Introduction | ix

Creation and Covenant of Works | 1
    Gen 1:1, 26–28, 2:15–17
    Hosea 6:7

Enters a Snake | 9
    Gen 3:1

Creating Doubt and Distrust | 16
    Gen 3:1–5

The Ruin and Judgment of Mankind | 25
    Gen 3:6–13, 16–19

The Covenant of Grace | 37
    Gen 3:14–15, 20–21

Paradise Lost, Paradise Restored | 49
    Gen 3:22–24
    Rev 22:1–5

Christ Jesus, the Spirit of Prophecy, the
    Centerpiece of all Covenants | 55
    Gen 3:15
    Rev 19:10
    Luke 24:25–27

Bibliography | 69

Introduction

ONCE UPON A TIME there was a powerful king who graciously ruled over a great land. This land was filled with inexhaustible beauty unparalleled in other lands. The king loved to walk in the land amongst its inhabitants, taking in the beauty of his kingdom. He sent a messenger to deliver good tidings to the inhabitants of the land proclaiming to them that as long as they obeyed the law of the land and cultivated the beauty of the kingdom over all lands they would be blessed beyond measure. All needs and delights ever before them would overflow forever. Most importantly the king himself would dwell amongst them in friendship. Peace reigned in the land and untold prosperity. However, over time the inhabitants of the land grew greedy. They desired to be more than subjects to this gracious king. They wanted the land for themselves. To be governed by their own ideas. To live lives their own way. Therefore, they rebelled. The consequences of their actions were swift. Soon it became clear that their ideas lead to chaos, devastation, and destruction for the law of king was for their good. The once beautiful land now bore the ravages of human pride and selfishness. The once beautiful kingdom fell into ruin, devastation, and war. The king in great mercy sent out another decree by way of a messenger. All who repent and submit to the king's son, who was to take up residence in the land, would be forgiven of their trespass. Loyalty to the coming king's son would result in the restoration of friendship with the king and the bestowal of his abundant provision for ages to come. All who would not repent of their treason would be barred from the land and destroyed by the king's army. Most in the land rejected the kings offer, believing themselves and the ruined world to be better than what the king offered. Yet there was a few compelled to repent upon seeing the error of their ways, the goodness of the king and his righteous reign. They accepted the terms of the decree and looked forward to the son of the king to dwell in the land, which would bring the fullness of the offer to bear on them.

Now imagine if the king's two messages in this story had not been told rightly. Imagine if the first agreement had not been conveyed correctly or the second agreement of grace had not been proclaimed as delivered by the king. Would not the messengers bear reproach before the king to have not delivered the edicts of the king, the covenants of the king to his people. The covenants themselves were given by the king. The messenger was to deliver it, not change it because of fear that the majority of the inhabitants of the land would reject its terms. The messengers were not to change, soften, or redefine the terms of the edict. For if the messenger changed the terms would not the king still destroy the land and its inhabitants for their rebellion? A judgment they deserved. Would not the king punish the messengers who failed to convey the edict as dictated by the king? Would not access to the glorious offer of grace be kept from the inhabitants? The message of the king gave rebels access to great grace. The message of Scripture does this very thing today.

This book seeks to give a primer for all those who are interested in the King of Glory's covenants with mankind from the opening chapters of Genesis, outlining God's terms to mankind. The whole aim of *Ruin and Redemption* is to examine the two overarching covenants that God sent to mankind as seen in Genesis 2–3. This book will endeavor to study Adam's, and all humanity represented by Adam, rejection of the first covenant, namely the covenant of works. Yet to see the offer of grace and the promise of redemption (covenant of grace) by the King of Glory in Genesis 3:14–15, which finds its fulfilment in the coming of God the Son into human history. The reason this book, I believe, will be helpful is in our time it is difficult to find a primer on this topic. Most of these things are written and studied well, yet the writing of such things lay primarily (not wholly, though) with the academic world. The Bible and its truths are a blessing to God's people and this book serves as an introduction to the covenant of works and the covenant of grace.

Also, this book will seek to examine that which flows out of and into the covenants from Genesis 2–3 namely: the temptation of man, man's fall, paradise lost, and paradise to be restored. Lastly, the aim of this book is to behold the One who brings the fullness of the covenant of grace, namely the Son sent by the King of the cosmos. John Flavel, a seventeenth century minister, wrote:

> There is nothing like love to draw love. When Christ was lifted up upon the cross he gave such a glorious demonstration of the strength of his love to sinners, as one would think should draw love from the hardest heart that ever lodged in a sinner's breast.[1]

May the centerpiece of the covenant of grace, the gospel of God the Father, draw your love and loyalty to his Son!

1. Flavel, *None But Jesus*, 84.

Creation and Covenant of Works

¹:¹ In the beginning, God created the heavens and the earth.

¹:²⁶ Then God said, "Let us make man in our image, after our likeness. And let them have dominion over the fish of the sea and over the birds of the heavens and over the livestock and over all the earth and over every creeping thing that creeps on the earth."
²⁷ So God created man in his own image,
in the image of God he created him;
male and female he created them.
²⁸ And God blessed them. And God said to them, "Be fruitful and multiply and fill the earth and subdue it, and have dominion over the fish of the sea and over the birds of the heavens and over every living thing that moves on the earth."

²:¹⁵ The Lord God took the man and put him in the garden of Eden to work it and keep it. ¹⁶ And the Lord God commanded the man, saying, "You may surely eat of every tree of the garden, ¹⁷ but of the tree of the knowledge of good and evil you shall not eat, for in the day that you eat of it you shall surely die."

GEN 1:1, 26–28, 2:15–17[1]

---

1. All Scripture is from the English Standard Version (ESV) unless otherwise noted.

⁷ But like Adam they transgressed the covenant;
there they dealt faithlessly with me.

HOSEA 6:7

TRY TO THINK ABOUT nothing for a moment with me. Even in this exercise you are thinking about thinking of nothing. We cannot fathom nothing. But God created everything out of nothing. He created everything that now exists by his Word. He spoke and all creation came forth. In six literal days God shaped the heavens and the earth for his chief creation mankind, who would reflect his image. Now, the flow of Gen 1 is quite precise. In verse 1 and 2 we read of God creating the heavens and earth while the Spirit of God hovered over the face of the deep. Day 1 God creates light (Gen 1:3–5). Day 2 God creates the heavens (Gen 1:6–8). Day 3 God gathers the waters and creates dry land on the earth as well as the vegetation and fruit trees to fill the dry land (Gen 1:9–13). Day 4 God created the sun and moon for the seasons of the earth (Gen 1:14–19). Day 5 God filled the waters with sea creatures and created the birds of the sky (Gen 1:20–23). Day 6 God created all the beasts, cattle, and livestock on the earth along with His chief creation man and woman in His image (Gen 1:24–31). Day 7 God rested from His work of creation, reigning supreme over the cosmos (Gen 2:1–3). Each of the days ended with the same formula "there was evening and there was morning" conveying that the day was a literal twenty-four hour period. Each day of creation was "good" except the sixth day which held the title "very good" in Gen 1:31. Why was the sixth day "very good"? The sixty day was very good because everything God created, with man being the climax, was especially pleasing unto Him. It conveyed His glory and mankind reflected His image. It is not significant that God declared after each day in Gen 1 that His creation was good until he made man and woman in His image and then he declared that His creation was "very good". "Very good" expresses God's delight in a creature that reflects back to him His own glory in a limited yet profound manner. Matthew Henry wrote:

> Of each day's work (except the second) it was said that
> it was good, but now, it is very good. For, now man was

made, who was the chief of the ways of God, who was designed to be the visible image of the Creator's glory and the mouth of the creation in his praises. Now all was made; every part was good, but all together very good.[2]

Henry conveys the intent of Moses in Gen 1:31 to point out that man was the pinnacle of God's creation because man was the one part of God's creation that best glorified God in its created state. Mankind reflected back to God His image. Just as a statue of an emperor reflects to the emperor who he is in his power and what he is like as the emperor of Rome, so did man in creation reflect back to God his communicable attributes (share with God on limited basis). This is what is called the *Imago Dei*, which is Latin for "image of God."

Imago Dei

What gives man his worth? What gives a human being worth, and what separates us from all of God's other creatures? Per the Holy Scriptures it is the *Imago Dei*, the image of God we bear. God made man and women in His image per Gen 1:26–27. Wrapped up in the word "image" and "likeness" is the worth of human beings beyond all of God's other creation. Concerning the word "image" in verse 27 and "likeness" in verse 26, one commentator wrote:

> The Hebrew word "image" (*selem*) refers to a representation, image, or likeness; it often refers to the way that an idol represented a god. "Likeness" (*demut*) means "similar in appearance," usually visual appearance, but it can also refer to audible similarity. Taken together, "likeness" complements "image" to mean that man is more than a mere image; he is a likeness of God.[3]

Charles Hodge stated in his work *Systematic Theology*:

---

2. Henry, *Matthew Henry's Commentary*, 7.

3. Johnson, *Image of God*, 806.

According to the Reformed theologians and the majority of the theologians of other divisions of the Church, man's likeness to God included the following points:

His intellectual and moral nature. God is a Spirit, the human soul is a spirit. The essential attributes of a spirit are reason, conscience, and will. A spirit is a rational, moral, and therefore also, a free agent. In making man after his own image, therefore, God endowed him with those attributes which belong to his own nature as a spirit. Man is thereby distinguished from all other inhabitants of this world, and raised immeasurably above them.[4]

The Reformed position, as posited by Hodge and others, defines the image of God around the reality of the rational nature of man's soul as well as the position of man in the garden. Man in the garden was given by God dominion over the earth under God's authority (Gen 1:28). The image of God in its fullness is tied to the Divine Commission given to Adam and Eve as well as the Divine Command that was to govern Adam and Eve in the garden.

The Divine Commission

The commission of God to man is clearly conveyed in Gen 1:28 "And God blessed them. And God said to them, 'Be fruitful and multiply and fill the earth and subdue it, and have dominion over the fish of the sea and over the birds of the heavens and over every living thing that moves on the earth.'" Notice clearly the charge given to man. First, be fruitful and multiply. To be fruitful and multiply means reproduce over the face of earth and fill the earth with those made in the image of God. Second, to subdue the earth. To rule the earth under God and use its resources for the glory of God. Third, have dominion over all that God made on the earth. Man was commanded to steward and care for everything that lives. Now man was placed in the garden of Eden, which we read of in Gen 2:5–14, with the commission to multiply, subdue, and exercise dominion. In essence, they were to cultivate the glory of the garden

4. Hodge, *Systematic Theology*, 97.

of Eden, paradise, in its beauty over the face of the earth for God's glory. John Calvin wrote with regards to mankind's authority that fuels the God given commission of man:

> He *appointed man, it is true, lord of the world*; but he expressly subjects animals to him, because they, having an inclination or instinct of their own, seem to be less under authority from without . . . .Man had already been created *with this condition, that he should subject the earth to himself*; but now, at length, *he is put in possession of his right; when he hears what has been given to him by the Lord*: and this Moses expresses still more fully in the next verse (verse 29), when he introduces God as granting to him the herbs and the fruits.[5]

Calvin commented on Gen 1:28–29 that God appointed man "lord of the world." Now Calvin does not mean man rules the world as God, but rather mankind is to exercise dominion over God's created world on behalf of God for the glory of God. Mankind is to care for the resources and spread God's glory in their image, in their multiplying in the world.

The Divine Command, the Covenant of Works

In Gen 2:15–17 God gives Adam one singular command by which to earn righteousness and live forever. The command being, "Do not eat of the tree of the knowledge of good and evil in the midst of the garden." Here, the covenant of works was established, and Adam received the command. Now, a covenant is an agreement between two parties that has conditions and requirements. One Bible dictionary defines covenant as "An agreement between two or more parties outlining mutual rights and responsibilities."[6] A covenant establishes a fellowship between two parties. In the covenant of works, Adam is required to obey the command which would have resulted in he and his posterity living eternally in perfect fellowship with the triune God. If he disobeyed, he and all in him would die

---

5. Calvin, *Genesis*, 96, 98. Emphasis mine.

6. Myers, *Eerdmans Bible Dictionary*, 240.

both spiritually and physically. He was commissioned to multiply in the earth and cultivate Eden across the world. The covenant was between the triune God and Adam, the first man of whom we all descend, as the representative of humanity. Adam was our representative before God in the garden of Eden, and the garden of Eden was representative of a temple, for that is where holy God and Adam fellowshipped together.

Eden was a temple in the truest sense for it was the place where God and man covenanted and met together in fellowship. It was here that Adam forsook the commission of God, transgressed the command of God and broke the covenant of works as implied in Hosea 6:7. Adam's failure and fall has consequences for all his seed in natural generation (descending from Adam through biological means). We all as mankind now inherit Adam's fallen nature and his guilt in the transgression of the covenant of works. In our country we elect representatives who operate on our behalf in government. Our representatives' actions and decisions affect our lives. Adam as our first parent and representative in the covenant of works with God made a choice that affects all generations to come that he represented before God in Eden.

The Westminster on the Covenant of Works

The Westminster Confession of Faith outlined the covenant of works in Chapter 7 Section 1 and 2. The confession states:

> Section I.—The distance between God and the creature is so great, that although reasonable creatures do owe obedience unto him as their Creator, yet they could never have any fruition of him as their blessedness and reward, but by some voluntary condescension on God's part, which he hath been pleased to express by way of covenant.

> Section II.—*The first covenant made with man was a covenant of works, wherein life was promised to Adam, and in him to his posterity, upon condition of perfect and personal obedience.*[7]

7. Hodge, *Commentary on the Confession of Faith*, 167. Emphasis mine.

Per Archibald Hodge there were five underlining truths in the Westminster Confessions Chapter 7 outline of the covenant of works, including:

> (1.) Every creature is under an essential and unlimited debt to his Creator. (2.) But the fruition of the Creator by the creature is a matter of sovereign grace. (3.) God has graciously pleased to offer men and angels a reward upon condition they render an obedience to which they are previously bound. (4.) In this covenant Adam is the representative of his descendants. (5.) The promise of their covenant was life—the condition, perfect obedience.[8]

Hodge tied the covenant of works imperative to God's act of creation. He wrote, "The very act of creation brings the creature under obligation to the Creator, but it cannot bring the Creator into obligation to the creature."[9] God instituted the covenant of works with His chief creation, mankind, who was represented before him by the first man, Adam. Adam represented all who would come forth from him in natural generation before God. If Adam had been perfectly obedient, life would have been granted. Yet Adam, on our behalf, fell and henceforth we thereby incur his guilt and inherit his fallen nature. A nature that it is spiritually dead (Eph 2:1–3) and in opposition to the glory, honor, and commands of our Creator. God is the Creator and mankind's fellowship with his Creator is dependent on God's covenanting with us. This framework is crucial to understand the nature of God and His relationship to man. For just as Adam represented us in the garden, the Second Adam represents all those in union with him before God the Father forever. Where the Adam failed in garden, the Second Adam perfectly succeeds. The Second Adam represents before God all who believe on Him. A topic we will discuss more later. However, for now understand that being represented by God in covenant is foundational to understanding what Christianity is and what gospel promises are for all who come to God through faith in Christ Jesus, the true and better Adam. Romans 5:15 states, "But the free gift is not like the trespass.

---

8. Hodge, *Commentary on the Confession of Faith*, 10.
9. Hodge, *Commentary on the Confession of Faith*, 168.

For if many died through one man's trespass, much more have the grace of God and the free gift by the grace of that one man Jesus Christ abounded for many." (Emphasis mine)

Discussion Questions

1. How did God create all things?
2. What is the covenant of works made between God and Adam, the federal head of mankind?
3. What is the connection of God's work of creation to mankind's responsibility to God as Creator?

Enters a Snake

*³ Now the serpent was more crafty than any other
beast of the field that the Lord God had made.
He said to the woman, "Did God actually say, 'You
shall not eat of any tree in the garden'?"*

Gen 3:1

THE SNAKE ENTERED EDEN, and walked, yes that is right, walked
up to Eve (Gen 3:14). The serpent had one intention, one desire: to
see Eve fall into deception and Adam into transgression and ruin.
The serpent came to Eve (who heard the command from Adam not
directly from God as Adam had in Gen 2:16–17) and uttered those
infamous words, "Did God actually say?" The attack was clear. Is
God's word reliable? Did they understand God's word rightly? The
question was posed potently and clearly. Now, who was the snake?
Moses, inspired by the Holy Spirit, described the serpent as "more
crafty than any other beast of the field". The word "crafty" is the Hebrew word "'ā·rûm" and it means "prudent, shrewd, crafty . . . per-
taining to being tricky and cunning, with a focus on evil treachery."[1]
This serpent is depicted as a treacherous animal. A cunning beast
and a tricky creature, but what and who exactly is this creature?

1. Swanson, *Dictionary of Biblical Languages*, cv. "'ā·rûm."

9

Who Exactly Is This Creature?

Later in Gen 3 after the fall God, addressed the serpent and states:

> ¹⁵ I will put enmity between you and the woman,
> and between your offspring and her offspring;
> *he shall bruise your head,*
> *and you shall bruise his heel.*

He states that the serpent will have offspring and they will be against the seed of the woman's offspring. The serpent is a leader of those against the offspring of the woman, the offspring of promise. In John 8:44 the Lord Jesus makes it clear that those in unbelief belong to the devil, to Satan, a fallen angel and the first being to sin against God. John 8:44 states, "You are of your father the devil, and your will is to do your father's desires. He was a murderer from the beginning, and does not stand in the truth, because there is no truth in him. When he lies, he speaks out of his own character, for he is a liar and the father of lies." So, Satan is the father of lies per the Lord Jesus here, and the first one to lie. This traces his handiwork to Gen 3:1–5, where the first lie is introduced into material creation. Therefore, we can conclude that this serpent was either possessed of Satan or a visible representation of Satan.

In Rev 12:9 John wrote, "And the great dragon was thrown down, *that ancient serpent*, who is called the devil and *Satan*, the deceiver of the whole world—he was thrown down to the earth, and his angels were thrown down with him." The word "serpent" in Rev 12:9 is the Greek word *"ophis"* and it means serpent, snake. It is the same Greek word used in Gen 3:1, 2, 4, 13 in the Septuagint (the Greek translation of the Hebrew scriptures), which lends great support that Satan in Rev 12:9 is the ancient deceiver of the whole world depicted in Gen 3. This provides significant weight to the thesis that the serpent who tempted Eve was either an actual creature possessed by Satan or Satan being manifested in a serpent form. Either way it seems reasonable to conclude that serpent was indeed Satan. Other scriptures that may be helpful here are texts such as 1 John 3:8 and Luke 10:18.1 John 3:8 states, "Whoever makes a practice of sinning is of the devil, for the devil has been sinning from the beginning. The reason the Son of God appeared was to destroy the works of the devil." Luke 10:18 states, "And he said to them, "I saw Satan fall like lightning from heaven." Satan is presented from these scriptures as a fallen creature who sinned from the beginning. The word "beginning" causes the reader to immediately thing back to the creation of the world in Gen 1:1. Satan is the tempter of Eve. He is first being to sin. He is an angel that fell into ruin by his own rebellion and then tempted Eve and thereby Adam all to the ruin of mankind.

Why?

The question "Why?" is one of the best ways to really dig out answers, and it seems this comes naturally to some children. When a child asks you a question, and your answer perplexes them, they follow up with a question, "Why?" You give them support for your answer, but they are still not grasping what you have said and want more. Again, they respond, "Why?" Before you know it you are several layers into an answer and expounding greatly on the topic. The question "Why?" is helpful. Let us employ it here. Why did Satan fall? Why did Satan tempt mankind? We know Satan was created sometime before the material creation of the universe per Job 38:7. We know that he was created innocent, holy, and unstained with sin because God is not the author of sin. If Ezekiel 36:12–19 is to be interpreted as the author addressing the "being" behind the king of Tyre in his pride than we have further information concerning the fall of Satan. Ezekiel 36:12–19 stated:

> [12] "Son of man, raise a lamentation over the king of Tyre, and say to him, Thus says the Lord God:
>
> "You were the signet of perfection,
> full of wisdom and perfect in beauty.
> [13] You were in Eden, the garden of God;
> every precious stone was your covering,
> sardius, topaz, and diamond,
> beryl, onyx, and jasper,
> sapphire, emerald, and carbuncle;

and crafted in gold were your settings
and your engravings.
On the day that you were created
they were prepared.
¹⁴ You were an anointed guardian cherub.
I placed you; you were on the holy mountain of God;
in the midst of the stones of fire you walked.
¹⁵ You were blameless in your ways
from the day you were created,
till unrighteousness was found in you.
¹⁶ In the abundance of your trade
you were filled with violence in your midst, and you sinned;
so I cast you as a profane thing from the mountain of God,
and I destroyed you, O guardian cherub,
from the midst of the stones of fire.
¹⁷ Your heart was proud because of your beauty;
you corrupted your wisdom for the sake of your splendor.
I cast you to the ground;
I exposed you before kings,
to feast their eyes on you.

In verse 13 we read that this "being" was in Eden, and in verse 16 we read that he was a guardian cherub, or an angel of authority. In verse 17 we read of Satan's pride. Pride is the exaltation of oneself over God's will and commands. Satan's pride swelled up and it caused his ruin. The answer to the question of "Why did Satan fall?" is "the pride of Satan." The love of his own beauty. The desire for exaltation and adoration. He wanted to be like God. However, what sparked such pride in this "being" originally created in perfection?

What Caused the Swelling up of Pride in Satan?

What was the trigger? A trigger is anything that garnishes a response. What garnished the response of pride in Satan? What exactly was it? Did he come before the throne and just decide to rebel? We must be careful here not to go beyond the revealed will of God into the secret will of God. To enter into the secret will of God with speculative language can be greatly unhelpful and plainly defiant.

Jonathan Edwards, contemplating the revelation of God concerning the fall of Satan from Scripture, wrote:

> But when it was revealed to him, high and glorious as he was, that he must be a ministering spirit to the race of mankind which had seen newly created, which appeared so feeble, mean, and despicable, so vastly inferior, not only to him, the prince of the angels, and the head of the created universe, but also to the inferior angels, and the he must be subject to one of that race that should hereafter be born, he could not bear it. This occasioned the fall; and now he, with the other angels whom he drew away with him, are fallen, and elect men are translated to supply their places and are exalted vastly higher in heaven than they.[2]

Edwards believed that Lucifer was unwilling to serve mankind, and in his swelling pride he became the accuser of the brethren. He was proud in his position and beauty as seen in Ezekiel 36:17. Edwards goes on to state:

> And the Man Jesus Christ, the Chief, and Prince, and Captain of all elect men, is translated and set in the throne that Lucifer, the chief and prince of angels, left, to be head of angels in his stead, the head of principality and power, that all the angels might do obedience to him; for God said, 'Let all the angels of God worship him;' and God made him (being Jesus) first born instead of Lucifer . . . .Lucifer aspired to be 'like the Most High,' but God exalted one of mankind, the race that he envied, and from envy to whom he rebelled against God, to be indeed like the Most High.[3]

Edwards is conveying that the trigger of Satan's fall was likely, per the witness of Scripture, the covenant of redemption in the Godhead. Having learned of God's will for the second person of the triune God to become a man in history and for angels to serve mankind to God's glory, Lucifer with great growing pride deemed

2. Edwards, *Miscellaneous Observations*, 609–10.

3. Edwards, *Miscellaneous Observations*, 610.

it beneath his dignity to serve mankind. Whether the conclusion of Edwards and others is correct is difficult to determined, but the similarity of the words used in Scripture, such as "bright morning star" for Lucifer and then Jesus (Isaiah 14:12 for Lucifer, Rev 22:16 for the Lord Jesus) among other scriptures gives perspective, with scriptural support, to the possibility that the trigger to Satan's pride was God's sovereign plan in the covenant of redemption as well as angels created purpose to serve mankind. Satan's pride brought about his and a third of the angel's rebellion that led to their fall from God's grace into a position of utter destitution, damnation, and depravity.

Why do this against an all-powerful God? Did the devil not know who he was rebelling against though? Did he not know that God is all-powerful and all-knowing? Did he not realize that his efforts at rebellion were a futile waste? Edwards, in his writings, later goes on to address this as well from the truths found in Holy Scripture:

> Seeing the devil is so cunning and subtle, it may seem a paradox why he will endeavor to frustrate the designs of an Omniscient Being, or to pretend to controvert him that is omnipotent, and will not suffer anything but what is for his own glory, seeing that God turns everything he does to the greater and more illustrious advancement of his own honour . . . To this I say, that although the devil be exceedingly crafty and subtle, yet he is one of the greatest fools and blockheads in the world, as the subtlest of wicked men are.[4]

Just as the devil's rebellion is utter stupidity, so too is the slightest rebellion of any creature today before God. To not submit to the all-powerful, all-knowing, all wise God is utter foolishness to one's own happiness and position in life. Yet mankind, as sinful creatures, daily defies the God whom cannot be overcome and who will punish all rebellion fully and finally on the great day of his wrath. His judgment also appears temporally in time in space per his sovereign dictates. The snake slithered into the garden full of deception and hatred for those who dwelled in the paradise of Eden. His aim

4. Edwards, *Miscellaneous Observations*, 612.

was their fall and ruin. his foolishness was to think he could thwart God's sovereign purposes. Rather, his evil was used for the eternal glory of God and the good of God's people, a principle clearly laid out in Scriptures such as Gen 50:21 and Acts 4:27–28. Nothing in heaven, on earth, or under the sea happens apart from the decree of God. All is under his reign, even those in rebellion to Him. The snake entered into the garden . . . only because God determined to allow it. He slithered out awaiting his doom and destruction under crushing boot of the seed of the woman. A death blow to the serpent's person and work that would come in history.

Discussion Questions

1. What is the evidence of the snake being Satan?
2. What caused Satan's fall?
3. What was the possible trigger of Satan's fall?

Creating Doubt and Distrust

3:1 Now the serpent was more crafty than any other
beast of the field that the Lord God had made.
He said to the woman, "Did God actually say, 'You shall not
eat of any tree in the garden'?"² And the woman said to the
serpent, "We may eat of the fruit of the trees in the garden, ³ but
God said, 'You shall not eat of the fruit of the tree that is in the
midst of the garden, neither shall you touch it, lest you die.'"
⁴ But the serpent said to the woman, "You will not surely die.
⁵ For God knows that when you eat of it your eyes will be
opened, and you will be like God, knowing good and evil."

GEN 3:1–5

DOUBTING THE VALIDITY OF the word is God is the oldest threat to the covenant people of God. It is one of the greatest threats that local churches face head-on today and is as old as Adam and Eve in the garden. "Did God actually say?" is the attack that is used by many to create, as well as promote, unbelief. It is the strategy of our adversary in Eden and today. Today, the charge is propagated in a variety of ways such as did Gen 1 actually teach creation to take place in seven literal days? Did the Gospels truly capture what the Lord Jesus actually taught? Did Paul really mean Jesus is propitiation, redemption, expiation? Did Paul say really mean we are saved apart from works? This is a sample of questions being posed in some of the circles I have encountered. With question you can hear the whisper of the serpent's voice, "Did God actually say?" Other more subtle attacks include: "Did God actually say what we are to do in the worship of Him?" "Are we not allowed to worship God how we desire as long as it does not have an explicit command of God against it?" The same serpent's voice hisses in each of these questions. "Did God actually say," has wreaked havoc on the minds of men and women in all ages of history and is a continual threat to the Church's faithfulness and fidelity in each and every generation.

The Seed of Doubt Sown

When the serpent stated the words, "Did God actually say?" the seed of doubt was firmly planted in the soil of Eve's mind. The temptation to doubt what God had said was planted and would bear fruit in the serpent's later statements. The woman Eve, to her credit, initially corrects the serpent who asked her, "Did God actually say, 'You shall not eat of any tree in the garden?'" She responded with a statement that was filled with truth, though with an addition to the word of God was made by Eve. She stated, "We may eat of the fruit of the trees in the garden, but God said, 'You shall not eat of the fruit of the tree that is in the midst of the garden, neither shall you touch it, lest you die.'" She corrected the serpent, yet she also added to the word of God and thereby corrupted what God had said. God had never said she and Adam could not touch the tree of the knowledge of good and evil (Gen 2:17). God told Adam they could not eat of it, but touching it was not mentioned. Perhaps Adam or Eve added that as a safeguard. Regardless, the word of God had been challenged by Satan and the word of God had been added to by Eve. The seed of doubt was rooted deep in the mind of Adam and Eve. The seed of doubt concerning God's word was planted and now the serpent watered it to give it growth.

The serpent declared in Gen 3:4 that God's word was wrong. God surely did not mean that they would die. In actuality, in verse 5 taking of the tree was the path forward per the serpent's logic for the day Adam and Eve took the forbidden fruit they would be like God and know good and evil. The seed of doubt was thoroughly watered with a statement against what God said, a statement implying that God was withholding something good from Adam and Eve. This act by the serpent caused the seed to germinate and sprout forth the first act of disobedience in human history. The doubt of God's care, God's goodness, God's perfections, and the doubt that God would do as he said, namely bring them to death, wrought unbelief in the heart of Adam. The doubt of all that God is and said was thoroughly imprinted in Adam and Eve's mind by the serpent and Eve's faith moved from trusting God's word to the serpent's statements. All that was left for Eve to do was gaze upon that which she desired and Adam with her. They took the fruit and ate. Their eyes were opened experientially to evil in contrast to good. They knew they were naked and tried to cover their shame with man-made fig leaves before the all-seeing God. They fell into utter ruin, ruin that began in the hearts of Adam and Eve's disbelief of God's word.

Thomas Brooks in the book, *Precious Remedies Against Satan's Devices*, wrote, "Satan's first device to draw the soul into sin is, to present the bait—and hide the hook; to present the golden cup-and hide the poison; to present the sweet, the pleasure, and the profit that may flow in upon the soul by yielding to sin- and to hide from the soul the wrath and misery that will certainly follow the committing of sin."[1] The devil presented a gold cup to Eve filled with the poison of untruth. He hid the hook in the bait. Both Adam and Eve drank the poisoned golden cup, took the bait, caught therein by the hook. From the fall to our time today this is still Satan's primary strategy in the world of mankind. He offers us the cup of being our own gods. He casts the line with the bait of, "God is love and will not punish you." Mankind, in our sin nature, daily drinks the cup and takes hold of the bait, caught by the hook.

What is the remedy for mankind? The remedy for mankind is God's work in the heart by his Spirit to bring about faith in the Word of God. The object of Adam's faith was supposed to be what the LORD had said to him in Gen. It was supposed to be the anchor of his actions and the guide of his mind. Instead, disbelief of what

1. Brooks, *Precious Remedies Against Satan's Devices*, Device 1.

God had said clouded his mind and moved his anchor to the bait of Satan. The result was the fall.

The Word of God's Promises is the Object of True Faith

About the word of God William Perkins wrote, "The Word of God is God's wisdom revealing from heaven the truth which is according to godliness."[2] The scriptures, all sixty-six books in the canon, are the inspired word of God given to mankind. It is the truth of God and it is to be basis of our hope. Its promises are yes in Jesus (2 Cor 1:20) are the object of our trust. True faith must have an object. This is clearly seen in Rom 10:13–17 whereby the apostle Paul writes the promise of God in verse 13 to save all who call upon the name of the Lord. This is a promise that will only be known by a person if he or she hears it proclaimed to them. Paul in verse 17 summarizes how true faith is only possible if it has the object of the "word of Christ." Notice the flow of the entire passage:

> [13] For "everyone who calls on the name of the Lord will be saved."
> [14] How then will they call on him in whom they have not believed? And how are they to believe in him of whom they have never heard? And how are they to hear without someone preaching? [15] And how are they to preach unless they are sent? As it is written, "How beautiful are the feet of those who preach the good news!" [16] But they have not all obeyed the gospel. For Isaiah says, "Lord, who has believed what he has heard from us?" [17] So faith comes from hearing, and hearing through the word of Christ (Rom 10:13–17).

Remember what Perkins stated concerning the word of God, which contains the gospel of the Lord Jesus Christ. Perkins conveyed that the Word is from heaven and the source of godliness. There is no godliness, no knowing God, apart from his Word. There is no opportunity for true trust that God honors apart from knowing the

---

2. Perkins, *Art of Prophesying and the Calling of the Ministry*, 9.

Word of Christ. With all this being true, it is evident that the greatest need in our generation, all generations, is to hear the word of God rightly expounded and heralded. Why? Because saving faith is not possible apart from the word of God as the object. One must trust in the person and work of the Lord Jesus as revealed in Holy Scripture to be saved. The reality of this truth in all its fullness is found in the pages of holy Scripture. Since this is the greatest need for mankind, the greatest threat is still the serpent's whisper, "Did God really say?" I would encourage you if you have made it this far in this book to stop and take a moment to ask: "Do I hear the word of God expounded rightly ever Sunday (Lord's Day)?" "Do I spend time in the Word?" "Is my understanding of the Word driven by what God has said or the golden cup of the serpent's poison?" "What drives my world view?" "Is it experience?" "Is it human philosophy?" "Is it family traditions?" The serpent's hiss, his golden cup of poison manifests itself in so many ways. Yet God's Word is timeless and it will endure every assault against its authority, achieving all of God's decreed ends it was sent forth to accomplish (Isa 55:10–11, Matt 7:17–18).

The Greatest Need

The greatest need of the human soul is to hear the word of God expounded, for in the word of God the Son of God and his work is expounded. Thomas Watson, in his book *The Ten Commandments,* wrote:

> How can people disregard the Word or be drowsy when the weighty matters of eternity are set before them? We preach faith, holiness of life, the day of judgment, eternal retribution. Life and death are set before you, and does not all this call for serious attention? If a letter were read to someone about a special matter wherein his life and property were concerned, would he not be very serious in listening to it? In the preaching of the Word, your

salvation is concerned, and if you would ever pay attention, it should be now.[3]

The greatest need for the human being is reconciliation with God, forgiveness of sin, spiritual birth, and eternal life (John 17:3). The only place to find truth on who God is, our state before the triune God, the person and work of the redeemer, the commanded response, and the hope of salvation is found only in the word of God. The primary theme of the word of God is the glory of God in person and work of the Lord Jesus, the object of true faith. Nothing is more important than hearing the word of God. Therefore, nothing will be more attacked and has been more attacked than the word of God by the enemy of our souls. Today this comes in all sorts of forms such as: casting doubt on the miracles contained in Scripture, to questioning the human authorship of parts of Scripture like the Pentateuch (first five books of Old Testament), and dismissing moral commands of Scripture by calling them cultural admonitions and not timeless commands, etc. Pastors are even encouraged to fill their speaking on Sundays with more stories, anecdotes, moral lessons, helpful tips, and other methods in order to encourage people and draw crowds. Gospel truths and commands are only thrown in at the end of sermons if at all. However, it is the word of God that creates the people of God. God has spoken in his Word. It is clear. May we ignore the serpents whisper, "Did God really say?" and cling with all our life to the word of God. For our very life eternally is at stake and our only hope is the truth that is within the vehicle of Scripture.

Why Is It the Majority Reject?

How is it that so many people reject the Word of life? Why is it so many do not see the precious promises of the word of God? How is it that mankind joyfully hears the serpent's hiss and openly rejects the word of God? Upon Adam's sin, as we will read about in a later chapter, mankind fell into a state of spiritual deadness, total depravity, and a state of utter spiritual blindness. As we look around

3. Watson, *Ten Commandments*, 109.

our world and notice that so many reject the word of God and its promises in Christ it is imperative to understand that this is what the Lord Jesus told his disciples would be the state of human affairs. The Lord Jesus in Matthew 7:13–14 stated:

> [13] Enter by the narrow gate. For the gate is wide and the way is easy that leads to destruction, and those who enter by it are *many*. [14] For the gate is narrow and the way is hard that leads to life, and those who find it are *few*. (Emphasis mine)

Notice the words "few" and "many." "Few" is associated with those who enter by the narrow gate and are on the hard path. "Many" is associated with the broad path that leads to destruction. We can expect that in this present evil age (Gal 1:4) the majority will be travelling on the broad way that includes all sorts of backgrounds and ideas, all contrary to the word of God. This way includes all different religions and even many who would claim to be a Christian of sorts. However, the hard path is through the narrow gate whereby a man or woman has to leave all the world and its goods behind to enter. The gate is Christ Himself (John 10:9). The path is hard because it is a life lived under the rule of Scripture which stands in contrast to all human philosophy and religion derived from fallen human thought (Rom 1:18–28). All who are on the broad way are blind to the glory of God in the face of Jesus of Nazareth revealed in holy Scripture. Just as a blind person cannot see the sun rise or set. Just as a deaf person cannot hear a baby cry or the sound of a shout of joy, all mankind apart from God's grace to give them eyes to see and ears to hear will never hear the joyous call of Christ nor see the rising sun of his glory.

Our Eyes Must Be Opened, We Must Be Raised From Death to Life

For us to see the truth of God's glory our eyes must be open to it. We are spiritually blind, unable to see. God must raise us from the spiritual dead for us to breathe the breath of faith continuously. This is the doctrine of regeneration. Titus 3:4–5 describes this process for us:

> **4** But when the goodness and loving kindness of God
> our Savior appeared, **5** he saved us, not because of works
> done by us in righteousness, but according to his own
> mercy, by the washing of regeneration and renewal of
> the Holy Spirit.

The doctrine of regeneration is the truth taught in scriptures like John 3:3, 6–8, Titus 3:4–5, Eph 2:1–7, etc., concerning the work of God the Holy Spirit to bring the beloved chosen of God to spiritual life out of their spiritually-dead state that all mankind shares in Adam. This work of regeneration precedes conversion and results in faith alone by Christ alone for salvation (Eph 2:8–10). God brings about all this through the means of the gospel preached and shared (Rom 10:17). R.C. Sproul stated the following about regeneration and conversion:

> Regeneration is the work of God the Holy Spirit as He su-
> pernaturally and immediately changes the disposition of
> the soul from spiritual death to spiritual life. Conversion
> is a result of regeneration. When we are converted, we're
> turned around and we move in a different direction.[4]

A way of describing this is, "to be born again" as the Lord Jesus put it to Nicodemus in John 3:1–15. He told Nicodemus that he had to be born again to see the kingdom of God (John 3:3) and enter it (John 3:5). The result of being born again was believing on the Lord Jesus and his sacrifice per John 3:15. Have you been born again? How do we know? How do we know if we are alive physically? The answer is we are breathing this very moment. Faith comes by hearing the Word of Christ (Rom 10:17). Are you breathing spiritually? Do you have faith in the object of Christ? Is Christ and his promises your hope? Does this truth drive you love God and his people (1 John 4), to see the kingdom, and to hear the call? Reader, reject the serpent's hiss, turn away the serpent's cup, do not take the serpent's bait, and plant your roots in the word of God. You must be born again.

---

4. Sproul, "What's the Difference?"

Discussion Questions

1. What was Satan's approach in the garden?
2. What is so deadly about the phrase, "Did God really say?"
3. Describe the importance of God's Word with regards to true faith.

The Ruin and Judgment
of Mankind

6 *So when the woman saw that the tree was good for food, and that it was a delight to the eyes, and that the tree was to be desired to make one wise, she took of its fruit and ate, and she also gave some to her husband who was with her, and he ate.* **7** *Then the eyes of both were opened, and they knew that they were naked. And they sewed fig leaves together and made themselves loincloths.*

8 *And they heard the sound of the Lord God walking in the garden in the cool of the day, and the man and his wife hid themselves from the presence of the Lord God among the trees of the garden.* **9** *But the Lord God called to the man and said to him, "Where are you?"* **10** *And he said, "I heard the sound of you in the garden, and I was afraid, because I was naked, and I hid myself."* **11** *He said, "Who told you that you were naked? Have you eaten of the tree of which I commanded you not to eat?"* **12** *The man said, "The woman whom you gave to be with me, she gave me fruit of the tree, and I ate."* **13** *Then the Lord God said to the woman, "What is this that you have done?" The woman said, "The serpent deceived me, and I ate."*

16 *To the woman he said,*
"I will surely multiply your pain in childbearing;
in pain you shall bring forth children.

Your desire shall be contrary to your husband,
but he shall rule over you."
[17] *And to Adam he said,*
"Because you have listened to the voice of your wife
and have eaten of the tree
of which I commanded you,
'You shall not eat of it,'
cursed is the ground because of you;
in pain you shall eat of it all the days of your life;
[18] *thorns and thistles it shall bring forth for you;*
and you shall eat the plants of the field.
[19] *By the sweat of your face*
you shall eat bread,
till you return to the ground,
for out of it you were taken;
for you are dust,
and to dust you shall return."

Gen 3:6–13, 16–19

WHEN ONE HEARS THE word "ruined" they may think of food that has spoiled and gone bad, or perhaps a piece of furniture or house item that is broke without the hope of repair. No matter what pops into one's mind, the core concept is likely the same. Something is broken and irreparable per human standards. It is beyond salvaging, and its original created intent is lost. When I think of ruined, I think of a t-shirt stained with some sort of salsa or food and there is no getting the stain out. The t-shirt bears the stains of my inability to meet my mouth successfully. The thought of ruin may also come into the mind when we see artwork that has been destroyed or sculptures that have been defaced and split into pieces. Such creations will never be what they were created to be. You may mend them but they will never bear the mark of the original creation the artist intended.

The Ruin of All in Adam

Adam and Eve fell into ruin upon their disobedience. Eve saw the fruit, desired it, ate it, gave it to her husband (her spiritual leader) and he ate it. From that point forward Adam and Eve were ruined. Their minds would no longer be fixated on God's honor and their wills would no longer be free to serve God and enjoy Him. They were now fixated on theirselves, their lusts, and their own pleasures. Their wills were no longer free to enjoy God, rather they were bound to their own ruined and fallen desires. They forsook happiness for misery and there was no going back by their own choices or power. They were ruined.

Ephesians 2:1–3 conveys the state of mankind rather clearly. Paul wrote:

> [2:1] And you *were dead in the trespasses and sins* [2] in which you once walked, following the course of this world, *following the prince of the power of the air*, the spirit that is now at work in the sons of disobedience—[3] among whom we all once lived *in the passions of our flesh, carrying out the desires of the body and the mind,* and were by nature *children of wrath*, like the rest of mankind (Eph 2:1–3). Emphasis mine.

Paul outlines the status of mankind rather clearly in Rom 1:18–32 as well. Yet it is in Gen 6:5 that we see one of the greatest statements concerning what happened to man because of the fall. The passage is God's diagnosis of man post fall, "The Lord saw that the wickedness of man was great in the earth, and that *every intention of the thoughts of his heart was only evil continually*" (Gen 6:5, emphasis mine). The phrase that rings out with potent force "every intention of the thoughts of his heart was only evil continually." Every intention, not some of his intentions, not that man is a mixture of good and bad, spiritually speaking, before God. The diagnosis was, and is, that man's heart was continually, without end, evil before the all-seeing God. Man is completely against the goodness and honor of God in his very inward being. *The Second London Baptist Confession of 1689* summarizes the result and state of mankind due to the fall of Adam:

> They being the root, and by God's appointment, standing
> in the room and stead of all mankind, the guilt of the sin
> was imputed, and corrupted nature conveyed, to all their
> posterity descending from them by ordinary generation,
> being now conceived in sin, and by nature children of
> wrath, servants of sin, the subjects of death, and all other
> miseries, spiritual, temporal, and eternal, unless the Lord
> Jesus sets them free.[1]

The confession here conveys that all the posterity of Adam from ordinary generation is now corrupted. All of Adam's offspring are now of a nature that is in contrast to the goodness of God, is separated from fellowship with God. One commentator wrote, "Ironically, when the human race, who had been created 'like God', sought to 'be like God' (vv.5–7), they found themselves after the Fall no longer 'with God.'"[2]

Fellowship with God Broken, Image of God Marred

Most, if not all, know what it is like for a friendship or relationship to go sour. A friendship begins with fellowship enjoyed. Then, something happens. Something is said or done that breaks trust, hurts one of the parties in some way, and breaks the relationship. Adam's act of rebellion broke the relationship that he and Eve enjoyed with God. Paul calls us in Rom 5:10 "enemies" of God. All of us in our own natural state inherited from Adam are conceived and come into this world in enmity towards God. David, in Psalm 51:5, wrote under the inspiration of the Holy Spirit: "I was brought forth in iniquity, and in sin did my mother conceive me." We, from the moment life occurs in the womb, are at odds with our creator. Paul later in Rom 5 wrote, "[12] *Therefore, just as sin came into the world through one man*, and death through sin, and so death spread to all men because all sinned" (Rom 5:12, emphasis mine). He also wrote, "[19]*For as by the one man's disobedience the many were made sinners, so by the one man's obedience the many will be made righteous*"

---

1. *London Baptist Confession of Faith, 1689*, Chapter 6, Section 3, 21–22.

2. Barker and Kohlenberger, *Expositor's Bible Commentary*, 11.

(Rom 5:19, emphasis mine). What Paul drove at is called the doctrine of original sin/inherent guilt. The doctrine of original sin teaches that we are all sinners because we all come from Adam. We inherit the guilt of transgression for he was our federal representative before God. All who come from Adam in natural generation inherit a sin nature from him and thereby are naturally lawbreakers, liars, and God-haters. We are part of the tribe of rebels that foolishly defied the God of the cosmos.

Mankind's *Imago Dei* is Marred

Adam's act of rebellion not only changed the status of their relationship, and ours in Adam, with God, it also reoriented their inward disposition. Adam and Eve who had been made in the image of God, now no longer reflected that image clearly, rather they were marred. An illustration that helps one to understand the effects of the fall is a ruined castle. Mankind is like a castle; once magnificent in its structure that over time fell into ruin and disrepair. Over time it became a monument to a past glory. The current condition of the castle prohibits any useful habitation. Reader, we as mankind are like that ruined castle. A marred image of the beauty and glory of a former time. We are ruined, but we are a magnificent ruin. We no longer reflect the moral attributes of God like we should. Our love is marred and selfish. Our justice is skewed. Our standard of truth and life is dominated by the love of pleasure, applause, or power. The attributes that we bear are marred.

What About My Free Will?

Often the question is posed in response to this idea that mankind is ruined spiritually, "What about my free will . . . I can choose God." The idea is this: there is an island of good in my heart that is capable of responding to God or I'm a mixture of good and evil. Imagine the picture of the devil on one shoulder and an angel on the other, both vying for the person to choose their way. Though prevalent, this idea of a will that is free to choose God is unbiblical and unrealistic. Remember once more what Paul wrote in Eph 2:1–3:

> [2:1] And you were *dead in the trespasses and sins* [2] in which you once walked, following the course of this world, following the prince of the power of the air, the spirit that is now at work in the sons of disobedience—[3] among whom we all *once lived in the passions of our flesh, carrying out the desires of the body and the mind*, and were by nature children of wrath, like the rest of mankind.

Per Paul in this text, our faculty of choice, the will, is in bondage to our sinful natures. Paul describes the state of fallen mankind as "dead in our trespasses, following the prince of the power of the air, living in the passions of our flesh" (Eph 2:1–3). This verse speaks of a person's faculty and ability to choose as being driven by the passions of the flesh and desires of the body and mind. He does not say that mankind is sick, and in need of medicine, but that mankind is spiritually dead, unable to know God based on their ruined nature and the will that follows it.

Mankind's will can freely choose horizontal things, such as, where to go to eat, whether to go to the gym, when to call someone, etc. However, mankind cannot choose God vertically because our will is in bondage to our own sin nature. There is nothing good in mankind that can respond to God. John 3:20 states, "For *everyone who does wicked things hates* the light and does not come to the light, lest his works should be exposed" (emphasis mine). Our desires drive our choices. Today I may desire to eat a hamburger with all the trimmings. This desire will dictate my choice to drive to a restaurant such as Burger King in order to purchase a Whopper with everything on it. My desire drove my choice. Our wills are not independent of our natures. Our natures influence and direct our choices whether we consciously recognize it or not. In Adam, we inherit a nature that is spiritually dead, with no spiritual good. We have natures that are only evil continuously (Gen 6:5). This nature is what drives our choices. This fallen nature is what our wills are in bondage to. We are conceived and born slaves of sin.

All mankind belongs to Adam naturally in their birth, and only those born again (born of the Holy Spirit per Titus 3:3-8, Eph 2:1-4, John 3:1-15) belong to the Lord Jesus who gives them life, righteousness, and justification (Rom 5:15-21). The Lord Jesus is the only hope of Adam's seed. We do not reflect what God is like as we were designed to do so. Not only are we ruined, but we are now under condemnation. We are cursed. We are under judgment. We are what is wrong with the world.

The Problem is Us

What in the world is wrong with this place? Have you ever wondered this as you beheld the crime and unrest in the world? Well, in short, the problem is us. It is we who are ruined and destitute of all true goodness in Adam. Perhaps you have bought the modern idea that you are a good person? Have you ever noticed people who say "I'm a good person" can only make that claim in comparison to others around them or in the society to which they belong? God's Word calls us not to compare ourselves to others in order to determine our goodness (2 Cor 10:12), but to compare ourselves to God's standard of righteousness. When we compare ourselves in light of God's standard the word "good" is the last description we can attach to ourselves if we are being honest examiners. You and I are wicked. The reason for abortions (murder of babies in the womb at any stage of development), sexual immorality, war, pestilence, famine, disease, heartache, hurt, and sin is the result, ultimately, of our existence in this world. Remember that in Rom 5:12 Adam, the first man, sinned and we inherited his sinful nature. It is natural for us to do things that are contrary to our good and to the glory of God. It comes naturally to us. It is easy for us. Per the scriptures, we sin because we are sinners. We are not sinners because we sin, rather, we do what is naturally in our heart. Rom 3:23 makes it clear this is the condition of all of us in humankind, not just some of us, but all of us. Rom 3:23 states, "for all have sinned and fall short of the glory of God." Your sin may manifest itself differently than others, however, make no mistake you and I are naturally rebels against our creator. Though some of our sins may be private and hidden, before God, they are ever present. God is holy and we are wicked. We all covet, lust, hate, manipulate, and lie, just to name a few. The reason for death, disease, famine, destroyed families, and hurt children is because we have hearts, apart from Christ, that are only evil continuously. We are the problem. However, to fully expand on this truth we must reflect on our creator so that we can see ourselves more clearly in light of his holiness.

God is Holy, Holy, Holy

In Isaiah 6, the prophet Isaiah is taken up to the throne room of God where his manifest presence is displayed. God's glory is brightly on display as Isaiah sees God lifted high and exalted. The angels are praising God in Isaiah 6:3, "And one called out to another and said, 'Holy, holy, holy is the Lord of hosts; the whole earth is full of his glory!'" Notice the angels are saying, "Holy, Holy, Holy." Holy means "other". The angels are singing the truth and reality that God is "other." They are singing that God is all together in a different category than all beings in the cosmos. God is the only being who is all-powerful, eternal, all-knowing, fully everywhere at all times, perfect in all his attributes. He transcends time and space. He is majestic and pure. He is perfect in all his attributes and self-existence. He is the source of all life. He is perfectly righteous and just. He does not change. It is God's otherness that brings Isaiah to the point of being totally undone. Isaiah falls on his face and says "woe to me, I'm a man with unclean lips and I live amongst a people who are unclean" (Isa 6:5). The first and foremost thing we must understand about how a good God interacts in a fallen world is to see that God's goodness and otherness is simply amazing. God is truly wondrous to behold. He is holy and good. He is the ruler of the universe, the Sovereign Lord. In contrast to his perfections our uncleanness becomes clear. There is no hiding it. The holy righteousness of God demands our sin be addressed in fullness because mankind demeans his honor and glory.

The Penalty of Rebellion

> [36] *Whoever believes in the Son has eternal life; whoever does not obey the Son shall not see life, but the wrath of God remains on him.* John 3:36

In John 3:36 we read the wrath of God remains on all who do not believe in the Lord Jesus. "Remains" is the Greek word, "*menō*" and it is a present tense verb which conveys that the action of "remaining" is continuous, unending, and unstopping. The word itself means to "abide, continue, to exist, etc."[3] The wrath of God continuously exists upon those who are not in Christ. That is the state before God that have always been in, are in now, and will be in unless they repent.

Now let us look at the word "wrath" to understand what is upon all those in Adam, all mankind, apart from God's effectual call to them. The Greek word translated "wrath" is "*orgē*" and it means anger or state of fury. It conveys that God's righteous anger, his just indignation, rests continuously upon all those outside of Christ. This is the state that all people are in from conception into eternity unless God should unite them to Christ by faith. The cause of God's wrath is the fact mentioned earlier that we bear the guilt of Adam (Rom 5:12–21) and are sinners in our very nature. God is perfect and his perfect justice demands that rebels be punished.

What is God's Standard of Justice?

By what standard? What is the standard of God's justice? In a just society the punishment fits the crime. Judgment follows transgression in equity. We see this principle rooted in the law of God. Exodus 21:23–24, "[23] But if there is harm, then you shall pay life for life, [24] eye for eye, tooth for tooth, hand for hand, foot for foot, [25] burn for burn, wound for wound, stripe for stripe." Eye for eye. Burn for burn. The context of the principle given in Exodus 21 surrounded men engaged in a conflict that caused a pregnant woman to be struck, which caused her child to come forth. This principle was to

3. Swanson, *Dictionary of Biblical Languages,* cv. "menō."

govern this case, and is the principle that is to be used to determine consequences of any case in the civil law of Israel. The punishment must fit the crime. It must not be too severe or too lenient. It must perfectly fit the transgression of the law. God's standard of punishment for those under his wrath is the same; their crimes must have an equal punishment. Their punishment must perfectly and completely match their crimes.

An Illustration: Same Crime Different Punishments

Justice itself also takes into account the authority of the one offended when punishment is disbursed. We see this in our society. For example, the punishment for assaulting a police officer is, in most contexts, greater than assaulting another person. The penalty for assaulting a governmental leader, like a president or prime minister, warrants a stricter punishment. Why? The offense, though the same assault across the board, each person being assaulted is not the same in authority. The higher authority, the greater the punishment must be. When we offend God, we offend the highest and greatest being in all the universe, the one with infinite authority and power. Justice then demands that the punishment be infinite because the crime was against a being of infinite goodness and authority. This justice will fully be dispensed at the throne on which Christ will sit over all nations, peoples, and creatures on that great day.

The Great White Throne

Judgment Day is a day that mankind inherently fears, the day when all sins are brought out and righteously addressed. The reality is, all who have transgressed God's commands, all in Adam, apart from Christ, will face the judgment of God. All transgression will be judged. We see this picture in Rev 20 and what a terrifying reality it paints. Rev 20:11–15:

> [11] Then I saw a great white throne and him who was seated on it. From his presence earth and sky fled away, and no place was found for them. [12] And I saw the dead,

great and small, standing before the throne, and *books were opened.* Then another book was opened, which is the book of life. *And the dead were judged by what was written in the books, according to what they had done.* [13] And the sea gave up the dead who were in it, Death and Hades gave up the dead who were in them, and they were judged, each one of them, according to what they had done. [14] Then Death and Hades were thrown into the lake of fire. This is the second death, the lake of fire. [15] And if anyone's name was not found written in the book of life, he was thrown into the lake of fire (emphasis mine).

Notice that all who stand before the Lord Jesus in judgment are judged by all the things written in the book of works. All of their thoughts recorded by God's all-seeing eye, all their wicked deeds, all their inaction when a just action was warranted, all their unbelief, cowardice, immorality, lies, slanders, murders, and impure deeds are brought out and then sentenced accordingly. With the sentence uttered by the Lord Jesus as judge, the punishment is then rendered as they are cast into the Lake of Fire, body and soul, to be tormented in the presence of the Lamb and his angels forever (Rev 14:9–11). At this point I would encourage you to authentically ask yourself if you have ever seen or grasped this side of God. He is holy. He is just. He will punish sinners. Psalm 5:5–6 states, "[5] The boastful shall not stand before your eyes; *you hate all evildoers.* [6] You destroy those who speak lies; the Lord abhors the bloodthirsty and deceitful man" (emphasis mine). Notice that the psalmist says God hates sinners. God loves his church and he is kind in his common grace to all the world. He gives man food and seasons in his common grace. The Lord Jesus states per Matthew 5:45, "[45] so that you may be sons of your Father who is in heaven. *For he makes his sun rise on the evil and on the good, and sends rain on the just and on the unjust*" (emphasis mine). The Lord Jesus defines God's common grace in terms of giving sunlight to evil and the good alike, sending rain on the righteous and unrighteous alike. God is kind to all sinners, but that is not the love of God that Bible speaks of. That love is reserved for his church, his elect (Eph 1:3). Paul in Eph 1:3–4 wrote about God's love for the church:

⁴ even as he chose us in him before the foundation of the world, that we should be holy and blameless before him. *In love* ⁵ he predestined us for adoption to himself as sons through Jesus Christ, according to the purpose of his will (emphasis mine).

Yet, God hates sinners (apart from his grace) per Psalm 5:5–6. He hates rebels. His hatred is a pure and perfect hatred against the rebellion of creatures that owe God the very oxygen that fills their lungs and the blood that runs through their veins. Psalm 11:5 states this reality this way, "⁵ The Lord tests the righteous, *but his soul hates the wicked and the one who loves violence*" (emphasis mine).

God's whole being, his soul, hates the wicked. God is not someone who exists for us, we exist for his glory. Yet, in our natural state each breath we breathe, word we utter, and action we take, there is a natural defamation of his glory. We inherit the guilt and sin nature of our first parent, and we are under the condemnation that comes with the failure of man to keep the covenant of works. What hope do we have? We are ruined. We are under condemnation. What hope is there for us? The answer is profound, yet humbling to the pride of man. Our only hope is outside ourselves. It is the covenant of grace. Our hope is in God who gave his only beloved Son to save all who believe.

Discussion Questions

1. What does it mean that we are ruined?
2. How does understanding the holiness of God affect the gravity of the fall of Adam and his seed into sin?
3. What is the judgment for our sin before God?

The Covenant of Grace

[14] *The Lord God said to the serpent,*
"Because you have done this,
cursed are you above all livestock
and above all beasts of the field;
on your belly you shall go,
and dust you shall eat
all the days of your life.
[15] *I will put enmity between you and the woman,*
and between your offspring and her offspring;
he shall bruise your head,
and you shall bruise his heel."

[20] *The man called his wife's name Eve, because she was the*
mother of all living. [21] *And the Lord God made for Adam*
and for his wife garments of skins and clothed them.

GEN 3:14–15, 20–21

AMAZING GRACE, HOW SWEET the sound that saved a wretch like me. I once was lost but now I'm found, I was blind but now I see.[1] These words come from John Newton's famous hymn, "Amazing Grace." This former slave ship captain turned Christian penned a profound portrait of his state, "wretch like me." Yet, the grace of God portrayed by Newton was stronger than the darkness of his

---

1. Opening lyrics from John Newton's hymn "Amazing Grace."

own soul and the severity of his wretched condition. John Newton is writing in "Amazing Grace" about the effects of the covenant of grace. Newton, a recipient of God's electing love and Christ Jesus atoning work, pens the hymn's finale focused on being in God's presence shining forth like the Son after which ten thousand years of such a state was stated to be "no less days to sing God's praise than when we first begun."[2]

The Covenant of Grace

The covenant of grace is first introduced in Holy Scripture when we read God's Word to the serpent who deceived Eve. God stated in Gen 3:15, "I will put enmity between you and the woman, and between your offspring and her offspring; he shall bruise your head, and you shall bruise his heel." Notice the phrase "the seed of the woman" for that theme will be repeated throughout all the covenants to come and fulfilled in Jesus who is the seed, or offspring, of Abraham per Gal 3:16. Also, notice that the seed of the women will be the one who crushes the serpent's head. This seed will undo the work of the serpent and its effects on creation. He will crush the serpent himself and will bring the serpent's judgment. This will come with a cost for the seed of the woman, for the serpent shall bruise the seed of the woman's heel. Later we see a picture of the cost when God slays an animal in verse 21 and covers Adam and Eve in their nakedness with the perfect animal skins of an animal that was without blemish from the garden of God. The covering of Adam and Eve required blood shed to atone for their nakedness. The promise of a Messiah was given, and his path clearly foreshadowed to bring the fullness of what would be the covenant of grace would bring.

The Second London Baptist Confession of 1689 states the following about the covenant of grace:

> (2) Morever, man having brought himself under the curse of the law by his fall, it *pleased the Lord to make a covenant of grace, wherein he freely offereth unto sinners life and salvation by Jesus Christ, requiring of them faith*

2. Ending lyrics from John Newton's hymn "Amazing Grace."

in him, that they may be saved; and promising to give unto
all those that are ordained unto eternal life, his Holy Spirit,
to make them willing and able to believe."[3]

(3) *This covenant is revealed in the gospel; first of all to*
Adam in the promise of salvation by the seed of the wom-
an, and afterwards by farther steps, until the full discovery
thereof was completed in the New Testament; and it is
founded in that eternal covenant transaction that was
between the Father and the Son about the redemption of
the elect; and it is alone by the grace of this covenant that
all the posterity of fallen Adam that ever were saved did
obtain life and blessed immorality, man being now ut-
terly incapable of acceptance with God upon those terms
on which Adam stood in his state of innocency.[4]

In section 2 of the confession we read a concise summary of the ush-
ering in of the covenant of grace. We read about its progression and
completion in section 3. Each covenant in history after the Adamic
Covenant is part of the covenant of grace. The Noahic Covenant is
part of the covenant of grace. The Abrahamic Covenant, Mosaic
Covenant, Davidic Covenant, and new covenant which is the covenant that fulfills all the others in the covenant of grace ushered
in by the Lord Jesus in his incarnation, life, righteousness, death,
resurrection and ascension. All the covenants in the Old Testament
are given solely because of God's unmerited and free grace towards
sinful man. They all include promises and conditions, but are all
of God's grace. They are all driving forward to the coming of the
Messiah who brought with him the fullest and final terms to dispense to humanity in the covenant of grace. *The covenant of grace*
is God granting eternal life to sinners who come to him by faith in the
promises of God that are fulfilled in the person and work of the Lord
Jesus. This is what was highlighted in Gen 3:15. Later in the Second
London Baptist Confession of 1689 the authors outlined the core

3. *London Baptist Confession of Faith, 1689*, Chapter 7, Section 2, 23. Emphasis mine.

4. *London Baptist Confession of Faith, 1689*, Chapter 7, Section 3, 23–24.
Emphasis mine.

of how God grants grace and forgiveness while also simultaneously punishing all inequity. Chapter 11 section 1 of the confession reads:

> Those whom God effectually calleth, he *also freely justifieth*, not by infusing righteousness unto them, but by pardoning their sins, and by accounting and accepting their persons as righteous; not for anything wrought in them, or done by them, *but for Christ's sake alone; not by imputing faith itself, the act of believing, or any other evangelical obedience to them, as their righteousness, but by imputing Christ's active obedience unto the whole law, and passive obedience in his death for their whole and sole righteousness by faith,* which faith they have not of themselves; it is the gift of God.[5]

How does God grant grace in the covenant of grace to sinners? What are the mechanics of this? The answer centers around the active and passive obedience of the Lord Jesus. This is the heartbeat of the covenant and the means by which God upholds his infinite worth. He in this covenant also grants his unconditional and free forgiveness to all whom he chooses, calls, and unites by faith to his Son, the Lord Jesus.

Active Obedience of the Lord Jesus

How did Christ bring the covenant of grace in it's fullness that we read about in the 1689 confession from holy Scripture? This is where we need to deal with the importance of the eternal God the Son adding humanity in the incarnation in order to usher in the covenant in its entirety. The incarnation is not just a nice story we celebrate every Christmas season. The reality of God the Son adding humanity in the virgin birth, to ultimately die on the cross, is the centerpiece of the covenant of grace. The Lord Jesus being truly God and truly sinless man (not through natural generation but coming forth from God the Father by the Holy Spirit in Mary's womb so as not to inherit a sin nature) is tied directly to how the covenant of grace functions.

5. *London Baptist Confession of Faith, 1689*, Chapter 11, Section 1, 34. Emphasis mine.

God the Son added humanity, not subtracting any of his deity, and lived under the Law of Moses, which republished the covenant of works requirements in its commands. The Lord Jesus lived under that law perfectly. Every action of the Lord Jesus as well as every attitude, every inaction, every thought, every motive was perfectly consistent with the law of God and thereby the will of God. The Lord Jesus earned a righteousness as a man that we as sinners in Adam could never earn. This is called his active righteousness or his active obedience. He actively obeyed and perfectly obeyed all the covenant of works' requirements republished in the Law of Moses without flaw or blemish. Where Adam failed in paradise, Christ succeeded in a dark world. Where Adam transgressed God's Word, Christ trusted God's Word. Where Adam sinned, Christ obeyed. Christ as the Second Adam, the new federal head for all who would be united to him by grace through faith, did all that is required under the law on behalf of his beloved church.

Passive Obedience of the Lord Jesus

The term "passive" means something that happens to you. The term carries with it the idea of a person receiving an action and submitting to it. The Lord Jesus obeyed God perfectly in his active obedience and submitted to God perfectly in his passive obedience. He submitted to the will of God the Father on the cross. He was crucified, bearing in his body the sins that were not His, enduring a penalty that he did not deserve, paying a debt he did not accumulate, and satisfying a wrath for guilt that was alien to Him. He passively submitted in perfect obedience to the Father's will, as the penal substitutionary atonement for God's people on a cruel rugged tree. This is called Jesus' passive righteousness, passive obedience. Perhaps the greatest place in all of Scripture to see the passive obedience of Christ painted for us to gaze upon is in the Garden of Gethsemane, moments before his betrayal.

Garden of Gethsemane

It was in the Garden of Gethsemane we are shown the depth of the Lord Jesus coming agony. He was not terrified of Pilate, Herod, the Chief Priests, the Sanhedrin, Rome, Satan, armies, and any physical suffering. He was troubled because he knew what the wrath of God was better than any being outside the Godhead could know. This was a wrath he was moments away from bearing not for one person, but for all the elect of God. Think about the Garden of Gethsemane when the Lord Jesus stated, "Remove this cup from me" (Mark 14:36) and "Yet not what I will, but what you will." (Mark 14:36, the entire Garden of Gethsemane accounts found in: Matt 26:36-56, Mark 14:32-52, Luke 22:39-53, John 18:1-11) Think about Jesus sweating drops of blood. Think of him in despair, calling out to God to take the cup from Him, yet submitting perfectly to God the Father's will. Christ Jesus was so torn, so shaken that even an angel is dispatched by God the Father to strengthen the Son. The wrath of God was terrifying to the Son of God. This should be the strongest of warnings to the world of mankind, namely God the Son feared the wrath of God so terribly because is truly beyond human comprehension has fierce this forever judgment is. Luke records this when he wrote:

> [43] And there appeared to him an angel from heaven, strengthening him. [44] And being in agony he prayed more earnestly; and his sweat became like great drops of blood falling down to the ground (Luke 22:43-44).

Yet, moments later at his betrayal when the mob asked for Jesus of Nazareth, he declared, with such power and boldness, that he is He, that they fell down at the voice of the Son of God (John 18:6). Christ's face was set like flint in perfect submission to the Father's will for him to suffer his wrath in the stead of all his church. This was the passive obedience of Christ that contributed to his active obedience that attained a perfect righteousness that no man from Adam in natural generation could ever attain to. The author of Hebrews in 2:10 wrote about this, "For it was fitting that he, for whom and by whom all things exist, in bringing many sons to glory, *should make the founder of their salvation perfect through suffering."* Christ being made perfect does not mean he learned how to stop disobeying, rather he earned a perfect record under the law every moment of every day in his active obedience and passive obedience through suffering and sorrow. He in his humanity earned a perfect righteousness and a flawless standing before God the Father.

What Is the Difference?

As a parent you know very well there is a difference between active obedience and submission. Active obedience is when your child knows your will and seeks to actively honor it and obey it. Submission is when the child knows they are to endure something like putting on that terrible Christmas sweatshirt from grandma and they submit to doing so. Jesus' active obedience was his perfect pursuit and obedience of God's will. His passive obedience was his submission to put on the wrath of God on the cross to save the people God the Father had chosen before time. In summation, his active righteousness is all that the Lord Jesus was and did in obeying all of God's will and commands. His passive obedience was his submission to the will of God the Father, particularly in the cross. Both of these are required for our salvation to work and the covenant of grace to be fully dispensed.

The Righteousness of God

The Lord Jesus is the righteousness of God that is required before God. It is his righteousness that is given judicially, imputed to the account of all who trust in Christ Jesus the Lord. It is the righteousness of Christ earned in the covenant of works, his active and passive obedience, that grants the possibility of the covenant of grace. Remember God is just, and only in Christ is God's justice satisfied and his mercy given. When a person is brought to God by faith in Christ the verdict from heaven "justified!" This person has the active and passive righteousness of the Lord Jesus imputed to them at the moment of their faith, for their sin was imputed to Christ who bore their sin, guilt, and curse in history almost two thousand years ago on a cross. Two scriptures where we see this wonderous dynamic are 2 Cor 5:21 and Gal 3:10–14. Let's examine both briefly.

> *21 For our sake he made him to be sin who knew no sin, so that in him we might become the righteousness of God.* (2 Cor 5:21)

> 10 For all who rely on works of the law are under a curse; for it is written, "Cursed be everyone who does not abide by all things written in the Book of the Law, and do them." 11 Now it is evident that no one is justified before God by the law, for "The righteous shall live by faith." 12 But the law is not of faith, rather "The one who does them shall live by them." 13 *Christ redeemed us from the curse of the law by becoming a curse for us—for it is written, "Cursed is everyone who is hanged on a tree"*—14 *so that in Christ Jesus the blessing of Abraham might come to the Gentiles, so that we might receive the promised Spirit through faith* (Gal 3:10–14). Emphasis mine.

Notice Paul's focus in 2 Cor 5:21 is that Jesus became sin who knew no sin. What sin did he become on the cross? He became the invisible (universal) church's sin. He took our sin and the punishment for it. He extinguished the infinite wrath of God for sinners because of his infinite worth. In Christ we, who are his by faith, become the righteousness of God. What is the righteousness of God in 2 Cor 5:21 that we become? It is the passive and active obedience of Jesus in his humanity that is given us before God in our judicial standing. The righteousness of God is the perfect keeping of the covenant of works by the Lord Jesus both actively and passively. Imagine with me for a moment a person who is penniless and in debt beyond what is ever possible for their position in life to repay. They are hopeless and destitute. Yet one day they come into the bank to discover that all their debts have been satisfied and their account now runs in the billions. They find out that the richest man in the world give them what was his and took what was theirs. Now their standing is all together different. Christ's death removes our sin debt and its requirements. His obedience is the merit that is transferred into our account before God. All we do to lay hold of this as God's elect is by God's grace to receive it by faith.

In Gal 3:10 Paul conveys that everyone is cursed who does not abide by all things in the law. The only way to have God's blessing is to do everything in the law of Moses. In Deuteronomy 29 the people of God are told the curses for disobedience to the covenant and the blessings for obedience. To break the covenant brings a curse. To obey, a blessing. Yet all humanity disobeys (Rom 3:23). This means all of humanity stands cursed in Adam. However, in Gal 3:13–14 we read that Christ redeemed us from the curse of the law by becoming a curse for us, namely, taking our punishment for Adam's guilt and our sinful breaking of the law of God. In Christ, the blessing of Abraham, the favor of God, the grace of God, and the Spirit of God is given to us because Christ removed our transgressions and gave us his earned standing through his human righteousness. This is the essence of how He, the Lord Jesus, fulfilled the covenant of works to grant the fullness of the covenant of grace to all God's chosen people. The covenant of works required perfection in obedience to God's command to merit eternal life. The Lord Jesus did this for his beloved church.

Cannot God Just Forgive Without the Cross?— The Great Riddle and the Great Exchange

I remember an objection being raised once. Well if God is sovereign and God is love than why does God need to send his Son to die a cruel death on the cross? Why not just snap his cosmic metaphorical fingers and forgive? Now, this objection is to God the Son's incarnation to die for sinners on a blood-ridden cross, which some skeptics would wrongly demean. The answer to their question is the reason God does not forgive apart from upholding his justice is because he is Holy and Perfect in all his attributes. In Exod 34:1–7 God's glory passed before Moses and God declared a profound but also puzzling truth about his perfect character. Moses heard God declare:

> ⁶ The Lord passed before him and proclaimed, "The Lord, the Lord, a God merciful and gracious, slow to anger, and abounding in steadfast love and faithfulness, ⁷ keeping steadfast love for thousands, forgiving iniquity and transgression and sin, but who will by no means clear the guilty, visiting the iniquity of the fathers on the children and the children's children, to the third and the fourth generation" (Exod 34:6–7).

God is clearly shown to grant mercy and forgive all the iniquity of his people, yet he is also shown to punish every single sin committed. How can these two truths about God exist at the same time? God is perfect in both his holy love and holy justice. Imagine a judge who is about to rule on a case. If he gives the criminal mercy than he has forgone justice for the crime committed. If he dispenses judgment and sentences the criminal than he did not grant mercy. In human terms mercy and justice are at odds. To grant mercy means justice is forgone. To dispense justice means mercy is denied. How does this work with regards to God who is perfectly just and perfectly merciful? This is where Paul's statement in Rom 3:24–26 is profound. Paul wrote:

> ²⁴ and are justified by his grace as a gift, through the redemption that is in Christ Jesus, ²⁵ whom God put forward as a propitiation by his blood, to be received by faith. This was to show God's righteousness, because in his divine forbearance he had passed over former sins. ²⁶ It was to show his righteousness at the present time, so that he might be just and the justifier of the one who has faith in Jesus. (Rom 3:24–26)

God is both the giver of mercy (justifier) and the dispenser of proper punishment (just) toward the one who has faith in the Lord Jesus. The Lord Jesus endures the justice of God, upholding his infinite honor and worth, in order to give the mercy of God. All sins are punished. Either we will face eternal judgment for our sin, or Jesus extinguished the judgment against our sin, removing our guilt, on our behalf by satisfying the penalty due to us (the church) in his infinite worth before God. God is perfectly merciful and just toward all who have faith in Christ Jesus. The character of God drives the Lord Jesus coming to fulfill the covenant of works in order to grant the fullness of eternal in the covenant of grace to God's people.

The Covenant of Grace Brings God Glory by Upholding God's Infinite Worth

When the Lord Jesus carried his cross and walked up to Golgotha, every step, drop of blood, shriek of pain shouted to all the cosmos, the heavenly host, and all creatures this is how much God's glory is worth in restoration. The infinite worth of the Son of God alone could repair the dishonoring of God's glory by sinners. The Son of God in his passion willingly conveyed to the Father the greatness of God the Father's worth by enduring all the pain and suffering, all God's indignation against sinners. The scene must have been shocking for the angelic host to see their creator humble Himself to such a degree. God's wisdom is shown and his honor is upheld in the cross of the Lord Jesus. Every part of the cross shouts the glory of God in righteousness upheld and love dispensed. God's sovereignty is on display. His power shown. His presence manifested. It is the moment in history that displays the glory of God to the highest degree.

Let us go back now to Rom 3:26 which states, "²⁶ It was to *show his righteousness* at the present time, so that he might be *just and the justifier* of the one who has faith in Jesus" (emphasis mine). God's righteousness is magnified. His grace is magnified at the same time in the cross. It is the wisdom of God on display to, in his perfections, uphold his honor that was demeaned by humanity and also to dispense unmerited, amazing, boundless grace to such rebels. God's glory is at the heart of the covenant of grace. Do you see it? Look no further than Christ Jesus incarnated crucified, raised, and ascended.

Discussion Questions

1. What is the covenant of grace?
2. What is active and passive obedience of Jesus?
3. How does the work of Christ uphold the revelation of God in Exod 34:6–7?

Paradise Lost, Paradise Restored

22 Then the Lord God said, "Behold, the man has become like one of us in knowing good and evil. Now, lest he reach out his hand and take also of the tree of life and eat, and live forever—" 23 therefore the Lord God sent him out from the garden of Eden to work the ground from which he was taken. 24 He drove out the man, and at the east of the garden of Eden he placed the cherubim and a flaming sword that turned every way to guard the way to the tree of life.

GEN 3:22–24

22:1 Then the angel showed me the river of the water of life, bright as crystal, flowing from the throne of God and of the Lamb 2 through the middle of the street of the city; also, on either side of the river, the tree of life with its twelve kinds of fruit, yielding its fruit each month. The leaves of the tree were for the healing of the nations. 3 No longer will there be anything accursed, but the throne of God and of the Lamb will be in it, and his servants will worship him. 4 They will see his face, and his name will be on their foreheads. 5 And night will be no more. They will need no light of lamp or sun, for the Lord God will be their light, and they will reign forever and ever.

REV 22:1–5

THE COVENANT OF WORKS was broken. All mankind represented by Adam in the garden of Eden, a temple itself, was plunged into ruin. All Adam's posterity is held guilty for Adam's transgression and inherits his sinful nature. A nature that is void of spiritual life and love. A nature that, without interruption or end, repels the goodness of God. God's response to such a fall was to remove Adam and thereby all his seed from the Garden of Eden. To remove them from access to the tree of life. In Gen 3:22–24 God removes Adam and Eve from the tree of life lest they take of its fruit and live forever in their fallen state of ruin and despair. God then places them outside the garden of Eden, outside his manifest presence with Cherubin guarding the entrance into the garden with flaming swords. The tree of life was barred from humanity. No access or entry was permitted. In no uncertain terms God conveyed to Adam and his seed that paradise had been lost. Life had been forfeited with the result that all the days of Adam and his seed would be spent in toil until to the dust mankind returned (Gen 3:17–19).

The Question

The question we need to ask is, "Why is this whole segment mentioned here in Gen 3:22–24 concerning God's internal thought?" Why is the triune God's internal conversation given to us in verse 22? Matthew Henry conveyed the ultimate aim of God concerning the expulsion of Adam when he wrote:

> The way to the tree of life was shut. It was henceforward in vain for him and his to expect righteousness, life, and happiness, by the covenant of works; for the command of that covenant being broken, the curse of it is in full force: we are all undone, if we are judged by that covenant. God revealed this to Adam, not to drive him to despair, but to quicken him to look for life and happiness in the promised Seed, by whom a new and living way into the holiest is laid open for us.[1]

---

1. Henry and Scott, *Matthew Henry's Concise Commentary*, cv. Gen 3:22.

Matthew Henry posited that the expulsion from Eden's ultimate aim was to convey to Adam and his offspring that entrance into God's presence was not attainable by their own righteousness from this point. Rather it must come through the promised seed of the woman (Gen 3:15). The internal conversation within the Godhead carries this truth to us. It was God's revelation to Adam, and all in Adam, that eternal life attainable through the covenant of works was lost forever by man's own efforts and attempts. We are barred from access to the tree of life, representing eternal life, by our own works.

Now at this point when people think of eternal life often just think in terms of the measurement of time. They think about not dying and living forever. However, that is not how God defines eternal life. Eternal life is primarily about knowing God, being in relationship with God unto forever. The Lord Jesus, in his high priestly prayer, prayed the following to God the Father, "³ And *this is eternal life, that they know you, the only true God, and Jesus Christ whom you have sent*" (John 17:3, emphasis mine). Eternal life is knowing God and Jesus Christ whom God sent. It is about being in fellowship with God the Father instead of outside fellowship with God the Father. This is why, per John 3:16, God the Son was sent into the world that all who "believe" in him "should not perish but have eternal life." The word "believe" is the Greek word "*pisteuō*" and it is a participle in the present tense, which means those who continuously trust in the Son of God. It is those who have eternal life the moment they enter this state of believing, which is a state that will not cease in this life. This state of believing is knowing God and Jesus Christ whom God has sent. Eternal life in is fullness, fellowship with God, is what was lost in the fall. Yet, we read in Rev 22 the fullness of restoration of the tree of life. The work of the seed of the woman was to destroy the serpent's work and bring us back into fellowship with God. In the last chapter of the last book in the canon of Scripture we read of the finalization of this reality for all who believe.

Paradise Restored

Paradise was lost and the tree of life was barred from humanity in Gen 3. But, in Rev 22:1–5 we see the tree of life mentioned once more. Now, through the seed of the woman, through the work of the Lamb, and through the covenant of grace in its consummation, the tree of life is given again to all those who belong to the Second Adam, the Lord Jesus. In verse 2 we read a marvelous description of the paradise of God once more given to man. Revelation 22:2 states, "² through the middle of the street of the city; also, on either side of the river, *the tree of life with its twelve kinds of fruit,* yielding its fruit each month. *The leaves of the tree were for the healing of the nations*" (emphasis mine). The leaves of the tree of life are for the healing of the nations. The nations marred with sin and death are healed and brought to wholeness. They are brought into the presence of God. If you continue reading in Rev 22 you will notice that the nations are brought to unhindered fellowship with God the Father and the Son, which we know from John 17:3 is the very essence of eternal life in its fullness. Read carefully Rev 22:3–5 below to see if you notice the emphasis of the apostle John's words as received from Christ Himself:

> ³ No longer will there be anything accursed, *but the throne of God and of the Lamb will be in it,* and *his servants will worship him.* ⁴ *They will see his face,* and *his name will be on their foreheads.* ⁵ And night will be no more. They will need no light of lamp or sun, *for the Lord God will be their light,* and they will reign forever and ever. (Rev 22:3–5, Emphasis mine)

Notice the phrase the author uses such as: "the throne of God and the Lamb will be in it," "his servants will worship him," "they will see his face," "his name will be on their foreheads," and "for the Lord God will be their light." All these phrases echo the essence of John 17:3 concerning eternal life. Eternal life in its complete and final state is knowing God and the Lamb without hindrance of sin. It is beautiful, sweet, unhindered, and perfect fellowship between a redeemed humanity and the triune God. This is the core of what makes the new Earth paradise.

The ultimate end of the work of the Lord Jesus in the covenant of grace is paradise restored, paradise being a restored perfect and unhindered fellowship with the Triune God. The Lord Jesus justifies all who believe before God the Father. He fulfilled the covenant of works on our behalf and took the penalty of our failure. He sanctifies us unto God by the Holy Spirit sent to indwell and seal us. Lastly, he glorifies us. He perfects us in his image and we, in Him, regain paradise. We dwell forever in his presence with joy unhindered. We read in Rev 22:3, 5 that those in Christ will dwell with the Father and the Son who is their light forever and ever. Paradise is restored.

Heaven

Heaven is often a topic that garnishes a lot of speculation from Christians. What Scripture conveys concerning heaven is profound. There are three aspects of our future as Christians that propels an existence of sinless and pure joy in the presence of God. First, Christians are perfected in soul upon their entrance into the presence of God at death (Heb 12:23). Second, Christian's bodies are raised immortal and without stain of fall or sin (1 Cor 15:35–57). Third, Christians inherit a new Earth that will never know curse or decay, an Earth that is filled with the glory of the LORD as the water fills the seas (Hab 2:14). When the Lord Jesus declared "It is Finished" before he gave up his Spirit in John 19:30, the victory He won was our justification. Yet it included all aspects of redemption for God's chosen people. Glorification includes our souls being made perfect upon our death (Heb 12:23). Next, glorification include our bodies being raised immortal (1 Cor 15:42–49). Lastly, it includes our inheritance of a new earth (Rev 21–22). All of this was won and accomplished in Christ's atonement on behalf of sinners who were chosen by God. The fullness of Christ's reward will be infinitely seen in the paradise regained and inhabited by all those in Him. Eternal life begins for the Christian upon God's grace to effectually draw them out of darkness into light, resulting in faith in Christ. They know God through Christ (the beginning fulfilment of Jeremiah 31:34) and this life eternal, as defined by Jesus Himself in John 17:3, only grows grander and sweeter as the believer grows in sanctification unto the climax of all that is in store for the life eternal of believers at the return of Christ and the resurrection of the believer. Do you have eternal life? Per John 3:16 all who are in the state of believing continuously in Christ alone have eternal life.

May the promise of Rom 10:13 bring rest to your soul reader.

> [13] For "everyone who calls on the name of the Lord will be saved" (Rom 10:13).

May Rev 22:1–5 bring an anticipation of joy that guides your present days on earth. Would encourage you to read it once more and mediate on its wonderous truths for all in Christ Jesus.

> [22:1] *Then the angel showed me the river of the water of life, bright as crystal, flowing from the throne of God and of the Lamb [2] through the middle of the street of the city; also, on either side of the river, the tree of life with its twelve kinds of fruit, yielding its fruit each month. The leaves of the tree were for the healing of the nations. [3] No longer will there be anything accursed, but the throne of God and of the Lamb will be in it, and his servants will worship him. [4] They will see his face, and his name will be on their foreheads. [5] And night will be no more. They will need no light of lamp or sun, for the Lord God will be their light, and they will reign forever and ever* (Rev 22:1–5).

Discussion Questions

1. What was lost in the garden?
2. What is restored fully on the new Earth?
3. What are the stages towards full restoration?

Christ Jesus, the Spirit of Prophecy, the Centerpiece of all Covenants

15 I will put enmity between you and the woman,
and between your offspring and her offspring;
he shall bruise your head,
and you shall bruise his heel."

GEN 3:15

10 Then I fell down at his feet to worship him, but he said to
me, "You must not do that! I am a fellow servant with you
and your brothers who hold to the testimony of Jesus. Worship
God." For the testimony of Jesus is the spirit of prophecy.

REV 19:10

25 And he said to them, "O foolish ones, and slow of heart to
believe all that the prophets have spoken! 26 Was it not necessary
that the Christ should suffer these things and enter into his glory?"
27 And beginning with Moses and all the Prophets, he interpreted
to them in all the Scriptures the things concerning himself.

LUKE 24:25–27

WHO IS THE SEED of the woman, the offspring of the woman that will crush the serpent's head? In Gen 3:15 we are introduced to the one who will bring the destruction of the serpent and its work. He is presented to us as the seed of the woman. In Gen 4:1 we see Eve longing for this promise and looking for its fulfillment in Cain. In Gen 5:29 Noah's father looks for the fulfillment of the promise in Noah being a prefigure to the seed of the woman. Abraham is promised that all nations will be blessed through his seed, and we learn in Galatians that this seed is Jesus Christ. In 2 Samuel 7 we see that this seed will come from the line of David. The seed of the woman is Christ, and in Christ all the nations who come to him by faith are blessed. Galatians 3:14, 16 spells this out beautifully:

> ¹⁴ so that *in Christ Jesus the blessing of Abraham might come to the Gentiles*, so that we might receive the promised Spirit through faith.

> ¹⁶ Now the promises were made to Abraham and to his offspring. It does not say, "And to offsprings," referring to many, but referring to one, *"And to your offspring,"* who is *Christ*. (Emphasis mine)

Christ is the offspring of Abraham, the one whom all nations will come to in faith and received the promised Spirit and life everlasting. He is the offspring of the woman. One of the most awe-inspiring realities as that this seed of the woman is also God the Son. The second person of the triune God. This is referred to as the doctrine of the incarnation. Per *The Oxford Dictionary of the Christian church*,

> The Christian doctrine of the Incarnation affirms that the eternal Son of God took flesh from His human mother and that the historical Christ is at once both fully God and fully man.[1]

Incarnation is a word that means the union of the eternal Son of God with sinless human nature through the virgin birth. The deity of Christ and the humanity of Christ are two distinct natures that do not mix to form a third sort of something. They are two distinct

---

1. Cross and Livingstone, *Oxford Dictionary of the Christian Church*, 830.

natures forever united in the person of Jesus of Nazareth (what is called the hypostatic union). The seed of the woman is the second person of the thrice holy God who adds humanity! The apostle John in his prologue to his gospel wrote this:

> [1] *In the beginning was the Word, and the Word was with God, and the Word was God.* [2] He was in the beginning with God. [3] All things were made through him, and without him was not any thing made that was made. [4] In him was life, and the life was the light of men.
>
> [14] *And the Word became flesh* and dwelt among us, and we have seen his glory, glory as of the only Son from the Father, full of grace and truth (John 1:1–4, 14, emphasis mine).

The Lord Jesus is the Word of God that was with God and is God and added humanity in the incarnation. He is the seed of the woman (Gen 3:15). He is the seed of Abraham and of David (Rom 1:3, Rev 3:7). He is truly God and truly perfect man, though not from natural generation. The Nicene Creed, which resulted from the Council of Nicea in 325 A.D. puts the identity of the offspring the woman as,

> And in one Lord Jesus Christ, the only-begotten Son of God, begotten of the Father before all worlds; God of God, Light of Light, very God of very God; begotten, not made, being of one substance with the Father, by whom all things were made. Who, for us men for our salvation, came down from heaven, and was incarnate by the Holy Spirit of the virgin Mary, and was made man.[2]

The offspring is the light of light, very God of very God. He was made man, though truly God. The offspring of woman is the point of all Scripture.

---

2. *Historic Creeds and Confessions*, Nicene Creed.

What Is the Point?

I have been asked, when critiqued by mentors concerning proper biblical preaching, "What is the point?" The idea of this question is to help one understand the message being communicated, to understand the main theme being expounded. What is the point of Scripture? In Rev 19:10 we read:

> For the testimony of Jesus is the spirit of prophecy.

The word "prophecy" in this passage is the Greek word "*prophēteia*" which means "an inspired utterance."[3] Inspired utterances are everything that God has conveyed, written, and stated. Inspired utterances are God's holy and infallible word. In 2 Tim 3:16–17 Paul wrote:

> All Scripture is breathed out by God and profitable for teaching, for reproof, for correction, and for training in righteousness, that the man of God may be complete, equipped for every good work.

The Scripture that Paul is writing about in 2 Tim 3:16–17 is the Old Testament, but what he is saying is true of the New Testament as well. The Bible is God-breathed. The Greek word behind the English "is breathed out by God" is "*theopneustos*" and it carries with it the concept of being inspired by God.[4] The Bible, the inspired utterances from God through human authors, per Rev 19:10 is all about Jesus. More specifically, "the testimony of Jesus" is the spirit of all prophecy. The word "testimony" in Rev 19:10 conveys the witness of Jesus and the content of Jesus that is the spirit of all prophecy.[5] The word "spirit" conveys the soul of prophecy, the disposition.[6] Jesus is the main point of Scripture. He is the fullness of his Father's glory. The author of Heb expresses this to us in 1:3 when he wrote:

---

3. Swanson, *Dictionary of Biblical Languages*, cv. "prophēteia."

4. Swanson, *Dictionary of Biblical Languages*, cv. "theopneustos."

5. Concept of "testimony" was read about in the following dictionary: Swanson, *Dictionary of Biblical Languages*, cv. "martyria."

6. Swanson, *Dictionary of Biblical Languages*, cv. "pneuma."

> He is the radiance of the glory of God and the exact im-
> print of his nature, and he upholds the universe by the
> word of his power. After making purification for sins, he
> sat down at the right hand of the Majesty on high.

The Lord Jesus is the main theme of the Old and New Testa-
ments, the point of all the Bible.

The Emmaus Road

Christ had been in the tomb a day. Sunday had come. Two of his
disciples were walking on the road to Emmaus from Jerusalem with
minds full of confusion and hearts heavy with sorrow. They had
heard that Jesus' tomb was empty, and a report of a vision concerning the resurrection of Christ was now circulating (Luke 24:22–23).
However, they may have thought in that moment the story was
just too much to believe. These two disciples of Christ were walking from Jerusalem, which was seven miles to the village Emmaus
(Luke 24:13). The resurrected Lord Jesus approaches them, though
they do not recognize Him. He asks what they were discussing as
they walked, and with sadness they told him (Luke 24:17–21). After they tell Jesus the story of the reported resurrection, he rebukes
them and states something profound. In Luke 24:25–27 the content
of his rebuke states:

> And he said to them, "O foolish ones, and slow of heart
> to believe all that the prophets have spoken! Was it not
> necessary that the Christ should suffer these things and
> enter into his glory?" *And beginning with Moses and all
> the Prophets, he interpreted to them in all the Scriptures
> the things concerning himself* (emphasis mine).

Jesus rebukes the disciples and points them to the law and all the
prophets (a way of saying the Old Testament canon) and then he
"interpreted to them in all the Scriptures the things concerning
himself." Per the Lord Jesus, the law and the prophets and all of the
Old Testament points to Him. It is all about his person and works.
He is the superior prophet, priest, and king. He is the sacrifice to
end all shadows and types found in the sacrificial system outlined

in Leviticus. He is the peace offering, the guilt offering, and the day of atonement. He is the Second Adam, the new head of a new humanity. He is the superior Moses who leads his people out of bondage through his blood on the doors of their life. He is the superior king of God's people, the greater and better David. He is the priest after the order of Melchizedek.

The Book of Hebrews: Exposition of Christ

One of the greatest examples of Christ being the spirit of prophecy, the theme of all the Old Testament, is conveyed in the book of Hebrews. The book itself was written to show Christ Jesus as superior to all the types and shadows of him in the Old Testament. The book conveys that all the Old Testament and its covenants centered around Christ Jesus and his work to come. The book expounds Christ from all the Old Testament. Below is a sample of several statements from this marvelous book with the Old Testament prophets, priesthood, and kingship as the backdrop by which the audience was to understand the Lord Jesus. As you read, focus on the statements in the italics to see how Christ is the centerpiece of all Scripture, the superior prophet, priest, and king of God's people. I know temptation here as well is to forgo reading these Scripture, but I would encourage you to reach each statement and mediate on them. Much fruit to the glory of God is produced in pondering holy Scripture with our minds.

Sample Scriptures from Heb 1–10

$^{1:2}$ but in these last days he has spoken to us by his Son, whom he appointed the heir of all things, through whom also he created the world. ^{3} *He is the radiance of the glory of God and the exact imprint of his nature, and he upholds the universe by the word of his power. After making purification for sins, he sat down at the right hand of the Majesty on high,* ^{4} having become as much superior to angels as the name he has inherited is more excellent than theirs.

2:9 But we see *him who for a little while was made lower than the angels, namely Jesus, crowned with glory and honor because of the suffering of death*, so that by the grace of God he might taste death for everyone.

10 For it was fitting *that he, for whom and by whom all things exist*, in bringing many sons to glory, *should make the founder of their salvation perfect through suffering.*

2:14 Since therefore the children share in flesh and blood, *he himself likewise partook of the same things, that through death he might destroy the one who has the power of death, that is, the devil,* **15** and *deliver all those who through fear of death were subject to lifelong slavery.* **16** For surely it is not angels that he helps, but he helps the offspring of Abraham. **17** Therefore *he had to be made like his brothers in every respect, so that he might become a merciful and faithful high priest in the service of God, to make propitiation for the sins of the people.* **18** For because *he himself has suffered when tempted, he is able to help those who are being tempted.*

3:5 *Now Moses was faithful in all God's house as a servant,* to testify to the things that were to be spoken later, **6** but *Christ is faithful over God's house as a son.* And we are his house, if indeed we hold fast our confidence and our boasting in our hope.

4:14 Since then we have a *great high priest who has passed through the heavens, Jesus, the Son of God,* let us hold fast our confession. **15** For *we do not have a high priest who is unable to sympathize with our weaknesses,* but *one who in every respect has been tempted as we are, yet without sin.*

6:19 We have this as a sure and steadfast anchor of the soul, a hope that enters into the inner place behind the curtain, **20** where *Jesus has gone as a forerunner on our behalf, having become a high priest forever after the order of Melchizedek.*

7:22 This makes *Jesus the guarantor of a better covenant.*

7:24 but *he holds his priesthood permanently,* because he continues forever. **25** Consequently, *he is able to save to the uttermost* those who draw near to God through him, since *he always lives to make intercession for them.*

7:26 For it was indeed fitting that *we should have such a high priest, holy, innocent, unstained, separated from sinners, and exalted above the heavens.* **27** He has no need, like those high priests, to offer sacrifices daily, first for his own sins and then for those of the people, *since he did this once for all when he offered up himself.*

8:1 Now the point in what we are saying is this: *we have such a high priest, one who is seated at the right hand of the throne of the Majesty in heaven,* **2** a minister in the holy places, in the true tent that the Lord set up, not man.

8:6 But as it is, *Christ has obtained a ministry that is as much more excellent than the old as the covenant he mediates is better,* since it is enacted on better promises.

9:11 But when Christ appeared as a high priest of the good things that have come, then through the greater and more perfect tent (not made with hands, that is, not of this creation) **12** *he entered once for all into the holy places,* not by means of the blood of goats and calves but *by means of his own blood, thus securing an eternal redemption.*

9:24 For *Christ has entered,* not into holy places made with hands, which are copies of the true things, *but into heaven itself, now to appear in the presence of God on our behalf.*

9:28 so Christ, *having been offered once to bear the sins of many, will appear a second time,* not to deal with sin but to save those who are eagerly waiting for him.

10:1 *For since the law has but a shadow of the good things to come instead of the true form of these realities,* it can never, by the same sacrifices that are continually offered every year, make perfect those who draw near.

10:12 But *when Christ had offered for all time a single sacrifice for sins, he sat down at the right hand of God,* **13** waiting from that time until his enemies should be made a footstool for his feet. [14] For *by a single offering he has perfected for all time those who are being sanctified.*

[10:19] Therefore, brothers, since we have confidence to enter the holy places *by the blood of Jesus,* [20] *by the new and living way that he opened for us through the curtain, that is, through his flesh,* [21] *and since we have a great priest over the house of God* . . . (emphasis mine).

What Is the Point?

In the book of Heb, we see that the Lord Jesus is the end of all prophecy. It all pointed to Him. In the new covenant, with the apostles as the foundation of the church and he as the cornerstone (Eph 2:19–21), all prophecy is complete. Jesus is the greater Moses, the superior Joshua, the true and better Adam. He is the superior and final high priest per the order of Melchizedek, an order of priesthood in Gen 14:17–20 with no genealogy which prefigured a priesthood that had no end. Jesus is the final sacrifice for sins and sat at the right hand of the Father showing his people that once and for all his sacrifice was sufficient to cover their sins, propitiate the Father's wrath, and perfect them in Him. Jesus, like Melchizedek, is a priest but also the king of peace and the hope of his people. He is the priest over the house of God, those who cling to the promises of God in Christ Jesus. He is the king of God's people. He is the fullest revelation of the Father's glory. He is the centerpiece of all the Old Testament. It is His, the Lord Jesus Christ's, shadow that is the Old Testament. Imagine the sun shining full strength against the object of a person and their shadow appearing on the wall they are standing in front of. God's glory is the light that shines. The shadow is the Old Testament and all its covenants. The person whom the glory of God shines upon at full strength is the Son of God. It is all about the Lord Jesus and his glory, his majesty, and his work. It is about the salvation of sinners who see their destitution per his law and thereby are effectually beckoned to look upon the prophet, priest, and king who alone can save them and bring them safely to the better and greater promise land. A land with no suffering, sorrow, or death.

In the New Testament we read of Jesus' life, ministry, death, and resurrection. In Acts, we read of his building the church through the apostles. In the epistles we read of who he is in detail, what he accomplished, and its affects in the new covenant. In Rev we read of his reign as king over his people and his kingdom's final consummation. The Lord Jesus is the point of the New Testament and Old Testament alike. He is the one the Father gives all things to for his glory. For as Paul writes of Christ in Colossians 1:16:

> For by him all things were created, in heaven and on earth, visible and invisible, whether thrones or dominions or rulers or authorities—all things were created through him and *for him* (emphasis mine).

All things were by God the Father through God the Son and all things exist for God the Son to the glory of God the Father. Jesus is the point of everything.

Hope For the Christian Reader: Contentment in Christ

Theology is always practical. A pair of glasses for those who are near-sighted makes objects at a distance appear more clearly. The study of God, theology, is not simply for the purpose of attaining great knowledge. The reason we study theology is so we can know the triune God more clearly and precisely. The whole aim of seeing the reality of God as creator, the covenant of works, and the covenant of grace is so that through those lenses we may then see the person of the Lord Jesus more clearly. It is my prayer that in seeing Christ more clearly you and I would love him more. It is my prayer that Christ's glory would fill our hearts and minds. He is beautiful to behold, and we behold him through the doctrines of Scripture. We do not want to be fundamentally big headed with small hearts. I am praying as I write this that these doctrines espoused in this book will be taken by God's Spirit and deeply rooted in your heart. I pray that you would find your heart strangely warmed with his glory and that your soul would fully enjoy contentment in Him.

Paul wrote in Phil 3:8–10 and in Phil 4:10–13 what knowing Christ produced in his life. He wrote:

> **3:8** Indeed, *I count everything as loss because of the surpassing worth of knowing Christ Jesus my Lord.* For his sake I have suffered the loss of all things and count them as rubbish, in order that *I may gain Christ* **9** and be found in him, not having a righteousness of my own that comes from the law, but that which comes through faith in Christ, the righteousness from God that depends on faith—**10** that I may know him and the power of his resurrection, and may share his sufferings, becoming like him in his death,

> **4:10** I rejoiced in the Lord greatly that now at length you have revived your concern for me. You were indeed concerned for me, but you had no opportunity. **11** Not that I am speaking of being in need, for I have learned in whatever situation I am to be content. **12** I know how to be brought low, and I know how to abound. In any and every circumstance, I have learned the secret of facing plenty and hunger, abundance and need. **13** *I can do all things through him who strengthens me.* (Phil 3:8–10, 4:10–13, Emphasis mine)

Notice the phrases Paul uses: "surpassing worth of knowing Christ Jesus," "I may gain Christ," "I can do all things through him who strengthens me." It is clear that Paul, in knowing Christ in the new covenant and knowing his (Paul's) failure under the Law, saw clearly the person of Christ. Christ was everything to him to such a degree that he proclaims all things are loss in compared to the surpassing worth of the Lord Jesus. In hunger or plenty he can do all things, meaning face all things, in Christ. Oftentimes Phil 4:13 is used in a way whereby a person strives to convey that they can do anything with their sports career, life goals, marriage, etc. through God who gives them strength. While some may be well intentioned in honoring the Lord Jesus in those things, Phil 4:13 is not about those endeavors. Rather, it is Paul conveying how he can face bleak circumstances and advantageous circumstances, and in all of life's trials and tribulations he can be content, which in this text means satisfied in the Lord Jesus. We see the context being contentment that is acquired in verse 11 when Paul states that he has "learned" in all situations "to be content."

The secret to Paul's contentment in Christ was God's power at work in him. Paul, in Phil 1:21, expounded to the Philippians that for him "to live was Christ" and in Phil 3:8–10 his aim in life was to know Christ. Paul wanted to know Christ and find his satisfaction in Him. In Phil 4:12 we see that contentment (satisfaction in Christ) was something Paul grew in and learned as a believer. Paul knew that God's grace was sufficient, and that Christ was more than enough for him in all circumstances. For Christ is the point of all things in the cosmos. He is the point of all of Holy Scripture. Only when a Christian gazes upon his glory from the Scripture are they transformed from one form of glory to another (Rom 12:1–2). Paul wrote in 2 Cor 3:18:

> And we all, with unveiled face, *beholding the glory of the Lord*, are being transformed into the same image from one degree of glory to another. For this comes from the Lord who is the Spirit.

God conforms his people more into the Son's image as they fill their mind with his glory revealed in the pages of Scripture. As they renew their minds (Rom 12:2). Christ Jesus is the sinless savior who atoned for his people's transgressions. The mighty king who loved his people enough to come and die for them. Christ and his love displayed in the cross draws the Christians heart to him where it finds its joy, rest, and contentment.

John Flavel, a seventeenth century minister, wrote:

> There is nothing like love to draw love. When Christ was lifted up upon the cross he gave such a glorious demonstration of the strength of his love to sinners, as one would think should draw love from the hardest heart that ever lodged in a sinner's breast. Here is the triumph, the riches of divine love; never was such love manifested in the world. Before it was none like it, and after is shall none appear like it.[7]

7. Flavel, *None but Jesus*, 84.

Look onto the love of God in Christ, for in Christ is all the riches of divine love and the triumph of the covenant of grace. Remember he is the one whom all things were created for. He is the point of all Scripture.

The Closing Question: Is the Point of Scripture the Point of Your Life?

Is the point of Scripture the point of your life? Is your faith placed in Christ and his covenant of grace? A faith placed anywhere else misses the very purpose of all existence. May God use this book in a small way to bring you to greater joy in Christ. May this discourse of the covenant of works and covenant of grace and the truths that orbit these two great themes in Gen 2–3 cause your heart to marvel at the one who fulfilled the covenant of works to establish the covenant of grace. Forgiveness and true happiness are only found in knowing this person, Jesus of Nazareth, through holy Scripture. The Lord Jesus stated in John 14:6, "I am the way, and the truth, and the life. No one comes to the Father except through me." He is the only way to God the Father. He, the person of Jesus, is the truth. He is life. May the treasure of heaven, the Lord Jesus, be our heart's treasure.

Discussion Questions

1. What does Rev 19:10 mean with regards to "the testimony of Jesus is the spirit of prophecy?"
2. How did Jesus interpret the Old Testament to his disciples on the Emmaus Road in Luke 24:23–27?
3. What is the point of the Old and New Testament and how does that influence your reading of holy Scripture?

Bibliography

Barker, K. L., and J. R. Kohlenberger III. *Expositor's Bible Commentary, Abridged Edition: Old Testament*. Grand Rapids: Zondervan, 1994.

Brooks, Thomas. *Precious Remedies against Satan's Devices*. New York: Scriptura, 2015.

Calvin, John. *Genesis*. Vol. 1. *Calvin's Commentaries*. Grand Rapids: Baker, 1981.

Cross, F. L., and E. A. Livingstone, E. A., eds. *The Oxford Dictionary of the Christian Church*. 3rd rev. ed. Oxford: Oxford University Press, 2005.

Edwards, Jonathan. *Miscellaneous Observations: The Fall of Angels*. Vol. 2. *The Works of Jonathan Edwards*. Peabody, MA: Hendrickson, 2005.

Flavel, John. *None But Jesus*. Edinburgh: The Banner of Truth Trust, 2018.

Henry, M. *Matthew Henry's Commentary on the Whole Bible: Complete and Unabridged in One Volume*. Peabody, MA: Hendrickson, 1994.

Henry, M., and T. Scott. *Matthew Henry's Concise Commentary*. Oak Harbor, WA: Logos Research, 1997.

Historic Creeds and Confessions. Oak Harbor: Lexham, 1997. Electronic edition.

Hodge, A. A. *A Commentary on the Confession of Faith: With Questions for Theological Students and Bible Classes*. Philadelphia: Presbyterian Board of Publication and Sabbath-School Work, 1869.

Hodge, Charles. *Systematic Theology*. Vol. 2. Peabody, MA: Hendrickson, 2020.

Johnson Jerry A. "Image of God." In *Holman Illustrated Bible Dictionary*, edited by C. Brand et al., 806. Nashville: Holman Bible, 2003.

London Baptist Confession of Faith, 1689. Apollo, PA: Ichthus, 2015.

Myers, A. C. *The Eerdmans Bible Dictionary*. Grand Rapids: Eerdmans, 1987.

Perkins, William. *The Art of Prophesying and the Calling of the Ministry*. Puritan Paperbacks. Edinburgh: The Banner of Truth Trust, 1996.

Sproul, R. C. "What's the Difference between Regeneration and Conversion?" *Ligonier*. https://www.ligonier.org/learn/qas/difference-between-regeneration-and-conversion.

Swanson, J. *Dictionary of Biblical Languages with Semantic Domains: Hebrew (Old Testament)*. Oak Harbor: Logos, 1997. Electronic edition.

Watson, Thomas. *The Ten Commandments*. Abbotsford, WI: Aneko, 2019.

.